Contents

KU-592-673

Acknowledgements

It is impossible to name all those who have helped in the writing of this book since they include everyone from former colleagues and pupils to critics of talks I have given and articles I have written. But I should like to acknowledge a particular indebtedness to Jonathan Croall, who originally suggested the idea and gave me support and encouragement throughout; my former colleagues on the Schools Council project Education for a Multiracial Society, for the use I have made of our common pool of ideas; friends within the National Association for Multiracial Education and the National Association for the Teaching of English, with whom I have enjoyed stimulating discussions over a number of years; and Carolyn Hawkins, who typed the manuscript.

Rather unusually, perhaps, I should like to acknowledge what I owe to three books on education which I read before or shortly after writing the book — Douglas Barnes's *From Communication to Curriculum* (Penguin), Mary Warnock's *Schools of Thought* (Faber) and Lawrence Stenhouse's *An Introduction to Curriculum Research and Development* (Heinemann). I am conscious also of the influence of the philosopher Karl Popper, whose work I came to late. Two of his central themes — problem-solving as a way of life and the 'open' society and its enemies — seem to me particularly germane for teachers in the multiracial, and indeed any, classroom. An 'open' school and an 'open' classroom, in which problem-solving is established as the prevailing method of teaching and learning, are long-term aims we should be directing ourselves to; the enemies who are likely to stand in our way are the same, *mutatis mutandis*, as those Popper identifies.

Sections of the book have already appeared in *English in Education*, the *Times Educational Supplement*, *Educational Research*, *Multiracial School*, and a Children's Rights Workshop pamphlet on children's books in multiracial Britain. Occasionally I must confess to having lifted chunks verbatim, but more often than not they have been reshaped or rewritten.

Introduction

This is a personal book. I do not mean that no one else has assisted in its composition (quite the reverse, as the preceding acknowledgements make clear), but that it is the expression of a personal philosophy and based almost entirely on my own eleven years teaching and working in multiracial classrooms. Naturally its content has been particularly affected by my most recent experience — two years as head of an English department in a small downtown multiracial secondary school with a white (partly Irish) majority. I am aware that had I taught in another school, a large comprehensive, for example, with a black majority, I might have had different things to say. Not that different however. The strength of my ideological convictions would have guaranteed a hard core of similarity. I thought I would save those who like to tease out writers' ideologies the trouble by coming clean about mine at the outset. I place myself firmly and unashamedly within the much maligned tradition of middle-class white liberalism and, as far as education is concerned, among the advocates of child-centredness which I take to be a manifestation of that tradition, although not everyone would agree.

The subject of the book is teaching and learning in the multi-racial classroom with special reference to the development of a multiracial curriculum. Its status is that of a discussion document — as carefully considered a contribution as I can manage to a continuing debate with myself and with others. It is not a definitive statement, nor (heaven forbid) is it intended as a *vade mecum* for those embarking on careers in multiracial schools. If I do have a tip to give probationers and students in training it is that they should beware all pedlars in pat prescriptions and solutions. But it *is* my intention to be practical. Since I address myself primarily to other classroom teachers, I have tried to anchor ideas, wherever possible, to classroom reality. I have also tried to bring theory and practice together, to form some kind of synthesis, by, in effect, setting the conclusions I had reached at the end of the Schools Council multiracial education project against two years of teaching to see how they match up.

As elsewhere in education, there are two debates about teaching in the multiracial classroom which are carried on separately and almost in defiance of each other. I am one of the privileged few to have participated in both. There is, first of all, the debate which takes place outside school and is dominated by LEA advisers, college lecturers, curriculum researchers, community workers and the like (the multiracial education lobby), and which directs its deliberations by and large to what schools and teachers should and should not be doing and to the effectiveness of different strategies for bringing positive influence to bear from outside. The second debate takes place exclusively in staffrooms. To some extent it is sensitive to the reverberations of the first, and suspicious and resentful of it too, since it perceives the multiracial education lobby to represent those who are comfortably removed from classroom reality and presume to compensate for their own earlier failures as teachers by regarding the profession as a suitable case for treatment.

Stereotypes and prejudices abound on both sides of the divide. Inevitably I have come to view those harboured by teachers more sympathetically over the past two years; perhaps I was predisposed to as well after three disenchanting years in educational research. But, although teachers are certainly justified in their scorn for a good deal of what has traditionally passed for educational research, their own attitudes are more often than not obstructive of development and reform. As a profession we are unduly closed, dismissive and cynical in our standard responses to new ideas; and unduly defensive and obsessive (not to say paranoid) about our dignity and standing. Sadly these inadequacies can now be found institutionalised in the teachers' unions. It should not be forgotten that real change, real progress, depend ultimately on us; they can only come from within.

Rightly or wrongly I have assumed a degree of familiarity on the part of readers with curriculum theory and with trends in multiracial education. On the former I should like to remind them of distinctions made over the use of the word 'curriculum' in the literature. Traditionally the curriculum is defined in terms of the learning experiences schools plan for their pupils. This is the curriculum of aims and objectives, rationales and syllabuses; the curriculum, in fact, of teachers' intentions. It has been called variously the formal, overt or manifest curriculum. Critics have commented that this accounts for only a fraction of what goes on in classrooms and of what children take away with them from school. Children learn also from the tacit beliefs and values of the school's 'hidden' curriculum — from the way they are grouped into classes, for instance, or discipline is maintained. Moreover what they actually learn in the classroom is dependent on more than teachers' intentions. Pupils have purposes too although they may not always articulate them fully. The 'effective' curriculum of what is actually learned results from the interaction between their purposes, their world, and their teachers'. This book has something to say about all three senses of curriculum — 'manifest', 'hidden' and 'effective'. I hope it is clear when I am using which.

The starting point for multiracial education is represented by some of the conclusions reached by my colleagues and myself at the end of the Schools Council project Education for a Multiracial Society and embodied in the project's as yet unpublished report *Multiracial Education: Curriculum and Context 5-13*. One main conclusion was that schools cannot begin to develop a multiracial curriculum until they have made a realistic assessment of the multiracial reality in which pupils are growing up. We identified racism, and its impact on both black and white children, as significant features of that reality. In so doing we found ourselves at odds with many classroom teachers who resisted the use of the word 'racism' and/or discounted its effects on children. Although accumulating evidence of the extent of prejudice and discrimination since then (the project finished in 1976) has somewhat eroded the resistance, the two debates (the staffroom debate and the multiracial education lobby debate) continue to define the situation in radically different ways.

For instance, in the context of the project's conclusion racism obviously means white racism. Understandably some teachers in multiracial classrooms resent the exclusiveness of this definition since their experience reports two pressing problems — racial hostility between blacks and Asians and the anti-white stances taken up by sections of the young black community — which the multiracial education lobby appears to disregard. Some participants in the outsiders' debate maintain that the second phenomenon, what teachers may well want to call black racism, is not properly racism at all, but an explicable, even healthy, reaction to bitter experiences in a hostile society; this claim, needless to add, infuriates teachers beyond measure. One facet of teachers' disgruntlement in the wrangle between the two debates is the complaint that the outsiders' analysis and the demands for action derived from it, are tantamount to an unacceptably 'political' intrusion into what should be a wholly 'educational' discussion. I find it extraordinary that the inseparability of politics and education should still have to be demonstrated in staffrooms. Decisions affecting who should be taught what, how, where and by whom are irrefutably political decisions. It was gratifying to discover the case argued recently with rare lucidity and cogency by a conservative educationalist, Mary Warnock, in *Schools of Thought* (Faber). As she deftly reminds her readers, 'democracy is a form of politics.'

Our second main conclusion on the Schools Council project was that the totality of what children are up against in a racist society demands from the school a total response. More is required than occasional or isolated multiracial inputs. If children are to be adequately educated for adulthood in a multiracial society, a constant and pervasive intervention across the gamut of everyday learning experiences will be needed which can be sustained from the beginning to the end of statutory schooling. We formulated this conclusion as a curriculum principle asserting that the regular curriculum should be 'permeated' with a multiracial 'constant'. Attractively simple as the idea of a multiracial policy across the curriculum seemed, we had to concede that it posed problems of implementation. It is not difficult to imagine how it might be realised in the ethos of the infant school with its integrated curriculum, but, in the case of the subject-based curriculum to be found in most secondary schools, it has to be admitted that the broad fields of the humanities and the creative arts hold out richer possibilities than do maths, science and technical subjects. In this book I confine myself even more narrowly in the practical chapters (four and five) to the business of teaching English in secondary schools. I hope that teachers of other subjects and other age ranges will find sufficient in the four remaining chapters to enable them to make the necessary translations. Again because of the inevitable limits in my own experience, I have little to say about the most vexed of all questions — given that one has achieved some success in one's own classroom, how does one then set about influencing the rest of the school? But I do sketch in a few thoughts at the end of chapter 6.

I want to devote the rest of the introduction to a brief description of my three years teaching in Kenya, because that experience was my introduction to the excitement and challenge of working in multiracial schools and it encapsulates some of the curriculum issues which were to preoccupy me after my return to Britain. Like others of my generation I went out to Kenya in 1967 for motives which were a mixture of the romantic and the idealistic. The white literature of the continent (principally the writing of Karen Blixen and Laurens van der Post) captivated me; and, in addition, I felt I wanted to do something for those less privileged than myself. Once there I had, of course, to face up to the harsh neo-colonial facts of life. I was confronted directly for the first time with the bitter legacies of colonialism and the vast and ever-widening gulf between the rich world and the poor. The colour of my skin necessarily conferred upon me membership of an economic elite and restricted to a degree I would never have imagined possible the nature and extent of my relationships with other races. Increasingly I asked myself what the government I had voted for so enthusiastically in the halcyon days of 1964 and 1966 thought it was doing supporting so generously a corrupt dictatorship (albeit a comparatively benevolent one by African standards), and how it could justify sending me 6,000 miles to teach children a curriculum so woefully irrelevant to their country's needs.

Despite these gloomy speculations I had cause to be grateful for the decision which posted me to teach English at a multiracial high school in Mombasa on the Kenyan coast. Founded after the First World War in honour of a famous nineteenth century Indian trader, Allidina Visram, it had until independence in 1963 exclusively served the Asian population of the town. The new Kenyan government, having enshrined multiracialism in its constitution, decreed that all former European and Asian schools should begin admitting African pupils. In 1967 the figure was stipulated as 50% of the first year intake; the following year it was raised to 65%. Given this percentage, the transformation of the school was quickly accomplished. By the time I left in 1970 most pupils were Africans, although the fifth and sixth forms remained predominantly Asian.

In 1970 the school population was as culturally diverse as any I have taught in. African pupils came from all over Kenya, Central and Western tribes being almost as well represented as Coastal ones. Most were speakers of Bantu language but some, like the Luo and the Masai, were not. The Asian children were mainly Punjabis or Gujeratis, but we also had some from the smaller communities — Goans, Baluchis and Kutchis. There were, in addition, Arabs and a large number of Swahilis (coastal people of mixed Arab/African descent), together with a few Somalis and Seychellese. Europeans were the only unrepresented Kenyan group. As for religion, a school survey undertaken by the fifth form in 1969 showed that one third of the pupils were Christians, one third Muslims and one third Hindus, Jains or Sikhs.

Educational decision-making in Kenya is, unlike in Britain,

firmly centralised. The transformation of the school had been brought about by direct government edict. It would have been reasonable, therefore, to expect the Ministry of Education to evolve through its inspectorate some kind of strategy, in the way of directives or suggestions, for the newly multiracial schools. No such thing happened. The reason was, of course, that the Ministry of Education defined the process it had initiated as part of the Government's general policy of Africanization. It was not a matter of developing a curriculum appropriate to a multiracial society, but of teaching Africans what had previously been reserved for Europeans or Asians. Certainly there were curriculum content changes, but these too were in the interests of Africanization. The Cambridge Overseas Certificate became the East African Certificate; African orientated geography, history and literature replaced the biases of Empire and Commonwealth; and Swahili was introduced as a compulsory school subject.

The thinking behind these changes was doubly mistaken; first, in confining change to content and, secondly, in believing that a black monoethnic curriculum was somehow better, more relevant, than a white one. African and Asian pupils were, in my experience, as bored by the comings and goings of empires and kingdoms in West Africa as they ever were by the power politics of Europe. More important, as far as literature was concerned, they were appreciative of cultural diversity and responsive to underlying human themes to a degree which the curriculum planners in Nairobi were either unaware of or discounted. Anyone who has ever taught English in Africa will report the extraordinary hold Shakespeare has over African and Asian children; there is no need to draw the local parallels with *Macbeth*, *Julius Caesar* and *Merchant of Venice* (three particularly popular plays), the children will do it themselves. Fortunately, being in Kenya during the transition period, I caught the literature curriculum at its most interesting point. For A level our four novels for study might be *The Mayor of Casterbridge*, *Anna Karenina*, *The Grapes of Wrath* and James Ngugi's* *A Grain of Wheat*, and our four plays *King Lear*, Brecht's

---

*When I took my sixth form to hear Ngugi give a public lecture in 1968 I might have predicted, from the gist of his talk, that ten years later he would have reverted to his Kikuyu name Ngugi wa Thiongo. I do not think I would have predicted so readily that he would be put in detention for telling the truth about the Kenyatta regime, in his latest novel *Petals of Blood*.

Galileo, Miller's *The Crucible* and Soyinka's *The Trials of Brother Jero*. Since then, I understand, the curriculum at both O and A level has become almost completely devoted to black (although not necessarily African) literature.

Even more regrettable was the decision to suspend the teaching of Asian languages in spite of the fact that in my school at any rate there were still the pupils and teachers to justify its continuation. Wrong-headed as I believed them to be, I was not entirely out of sympathy with the thinking behind these decisions. The call for a multiracial curriculum in Britain is related to a pluralist vision of the future of British society — a future in which racial minorities will be able to define their cultural identities in any way they choose. Whatever its merits here, in a country like Kenya, notwithstanding its separatist past, this vision is a political non-starter. Indeed, given the precarious state of Kenyan politics and the country's history of racial and tribal animosity, it could be argued that it would be tantamount to national suicide. The avowed aim of the Kenyan government, tirelessly reiterated at public rallies and in official pronouncements, is national unity. If the Ministry of Education had evolved a strategy for its newly multiracial schools ten years ago, the main emphasis, I feel sure, would have been on integration with a view to turning out good Kenyans dedicated to their country's future.

Left to determine our own strategies the school staff decided to re-examine organisation and curriculum in a series of sub-committees and staff meetings. In so doing we were particularly anxious about relations between African and Asian pupils. Relations between the two racial groups had always been poor on account of the privileged position enjoyed by Asian shopkeepers and businessmen, but they had deteriorated in the wake of the Kenyan government's Africanization policy and the British government's Commonwealth Immigrants Act of 1968. Tensions of this sort could be expected to find expression in the attitudes of African and Asian children, so, naturally enough, some staff regarded the Africanization of the school with apprehension, even though race relations in Mombasa and generally on the Coast were noticeably more harmonious then in Nairobi or upcountry Kenya where the Africanization of the former European high schools resulted in vicious racial fights.

There was more than just racial tension dividing our Asian and African pupils. There was also educational attainment. On leaving primary school Kenyan children take an exam which decides whether they qualify for secondary education. The Asian children admitted after 1967 were those who had excelled in the exam and put down our school as first choice. The African pupils, on the other hand, were mainly from the bottom end of the pass list, the more successful ones having opted for African boarding schools. The gulf in attainment was immediately obvious in Maths and the Sciences, where Asian children had traditionally done well, but was soon seen to apply to most other subjects as well. One reason for this was the Asians' immeasurably better control of the medium of instruction, English. Whereas most African children only had the English they had been taught (often inadequately) at primary school, many Asian children had a tradition of English speaking at home. Some even claimed it came more easily than their mother tongue and a few, the Goans and the Seychellese, were actually mother tongue speakers.

The educational gulf had its social counterpart. The Asian children were privileged by any standards. Most came to school on bikes and some were even chauffeur driven, while the Africans came by bus or on foot. The Asians were invariably immaculately dressed and equipped with everything that might conduce to success at school. The Africans could match them only in motivation; what many of them lacked above all was a satisfactory place where they could study in the evenings and at weekends. Even where home conditions were favourable their parents could offer them little help with their school work beyond encouragement.

The crucial issue turned out to be streaming. The school had always been strictly streamed and the usual arguments for and against its retention were adduced. One argument alone tipped the balance in favour of mixed ability. Streaming according to attainment criteria would have almost certainly left us, in a four stream entry, with one largely Asian class and three largely African ones (indeed this is more or less what did happen at the former Asian girls high school). It was generally felt that such a situation would have been intolerable, so the staff eventually found themselves in the position of teaching classes of 38 that were multiracial and unstreamed and contained in most cases, on the one hand, half a dozen Asian children of outstanding gifts and, on the other, half a dozen African children of very low academic attainment. It was also generally agreed that subjects of a more practical and technical nature should be introduced but the Ministry, with its elitist educational assumptions, refused to countenance such a change in direction. As far as they were concerned, the school's business was to continue, despite the radically altered nature of its intake, to secure good results in academic subjects. Nevertheless we were able to introduce agricultural science because we were fortunate enough to have a member of staff capable of teaching it.

Despite the imposed ideology of integration, and the abandonment of the teaching of Asian languages, we contrived to make some acknowledgement of the presence of minority cultures in the school, even if admittedly in rather token gestures. The different religions represented took it in turns to organise morning assembly; in any one week we might have readings from all the holy texts — the Bible, the Gita, the Granth and the Quran. Social entertainments invariably included Indian singing and dancing, and the problem of the school play, traditionally in English and therefore almost predestined to have a wholly Asian cast, was solved by having two — one in English and one in Swahili (in 1970 they were Sheridan's *The Critic* and Julius Nyerere's translation of *The Merchant of Venice*).

Although by the time of my departure the school was majority African, it remained quite distinctively Asian in ethos and character. This was partly due to the fact that the staff and senior pupils were mainly Asian, which gave the school a rather lop-sided feel and created, racially speaking, an unfortunate situation whereby non-African staff and prefects dominated an African majority. We tried to correct this imbalance by appointing African prefects regardless of whether in other circumstances they would have been regarded as suitable. The African pupils understandably found it difficult to accept the school as theirs. Unlike the Nairobi high schools it had not been required by the government to change its non-African name and they seemed to feel alienated from an institution which by and large they had not wanted to attend. The Asian pupils won all the academic prizes, except for Swahili, made up most of the school sports teams, except for football and athletics, and dominated school clubs and societies, even the Young Farmers Club, which had originally been established with Africans in mind.

The colonial inheritance was not the best foundation for a multiracial society. Nor was its educational system (or the one which replaced it) the best foundation for multiracial schools. Nevertheless the one I taught in was working after a fashion when I left. Certainly very little racial mixing took place, far less than in the average English secondary school, (it would have been astonishing had things been otherwise), but on the other hand we were bedevilled by none of the racial fighting and abuse which are such

commonplace features of the British scene. The staff can claim
some credit too for deciding to take a hard look at curriculum and
organisation in the light of the changed composition of the pupil
intake. I wonder how many British schools which went through
similar transformations in the 1960s had the imagination or
courage to do likewise.

The personal nature of this book explains both the autobiographical flavour and the informal style of much of what follows.
The school incidents and anecdotes quoted come from my personal
journal, which I have found such an invaluable aid to teaching
since I first stood in front of a class sixteen years ago. In the interests
of preserving anonymity I have sometimes altered details of name,
time and place, but the spoken and written quotations are authentic, and the incidents described took place.

1 Children and Race

'Black people came to our country. The question is will they stay
or go.'
11 year old white boy

'I would like to teach my children, if I have any, that they have
got a race and they belong to it.'
15 year old Muslim girl

Arguably the most important data available to teachers planning a
curriculum appropriate to a multiracial society are the racial ideas
and feelings children begin to develop before they first appear in
infant reception. An obvious enough proposition I would have
thought; yet it has proved eminently resistible to many, possibly
even most, primary school teachers, mainly (or so it seems) because
they find it hard to reconcile the research evidence on the evolution
of children's racial attitudes with their perceptions of their own
experience in multiracial classrooms. It would never have occurred
to teachers in multiracial Kenya ten years ago to argue that young
children were racially oblivious, but this is precisely the claim being
so widely made in multiracial Britain today.

Why the discrepancy? After all, although the complexion of the
racial majority may differ, Kenya and Britain are both societies in
which race has been and continues to be a highly significant factor.
The answer lies, I believe, in the romantic philosophy of the 'caring'
British primary school which defines itself as a bastion of love
shielding its pupils against the big bad world outside. It finds
confirmation for its sentimental colour-blindness ('children are just
children') in the fact, attested by scientific research and everyday
observation, that there is a higher incidence of interracial mixing
and interracial friendship among five year olds than among fifteen
year olds; moreover, in practice (such is its potency) the philosophy
has something of the effect of a self-fulfilling prophecy.

Before attempting to expose the philosophy's myths, it is necessary to summarize the research evidence into the development of
children's racial attitudes which has been gathered over the past
fifty years in countries as far-flung as the United States, Britain,
South Africa, New Zealand and Hong Kong and which British
teachers find so resistible. Briefly, what it reports (and it does so

with striking unanimity) is that children growing up in societies which accord racial minorities (in South Africa's case, of course, a racial majority) inferior status start to learn about the relative worth attached to being white or black at a very early age. The dawning of racial awareness at around the age of three is accompanied, or quickly followed, by simple signs of racial preference and rejection, and even five years olds are capable of commenting on the different social and economic roles fulfilled by different racial groups. The net outcome in a country like Britain is that white children will be predisposed to pejorative views of minority races which by the age of eleven or twelve may well have accommodated the familiar array of adult prejudices and stereotypes; and that black and Asian children will be predisposed to ambivalence about their racial selves which may, at worst, degenerate into self-denial, identity conflict and personality disorder.*

As part of my work on the Schools Council project Education for a Multiracial Society, I presented this evidence to a group of twenty primary and nursery school headteachers in a northern education authority where the racial minority is almost exclusively Indian and Pakistani Muslims. We met regularly at their local teachers' centre between November 1974 and June 1975 to examine the implications for the curriculum of living in a multiracial society. Rightly or wrongly, I decided that the opening session ought to consider the research findings on the early onset of racial attitudes, since otherwise the headteachers might underestimate what they were up against and settle for curriculum tinkering rather than the radical reform I believed to be essential.

All the nursery and infant heads, with one exception, and most of the junior heads rejected the findings as irrelevant to their own situations. In their schools, they insisted, matters were quite otherwise. Young children were unaware of race and the different ethnic groups mixed and played together happily. Where an incident did occur, it was invariably an isolated one and the result of a maladjusted child mindlessly mouthing what he or she had heard at home. This conflict between the scientific findings and the teachers' perceptions of their own situations left the group in an impasse which could only be negotiated by some kind of attempt at demonstrating who was right. So they decided to try to piece

---

*Inevitably this summary is somewhat crude. The full picture is more variegated and complex. Readers unfamiliar with the research evidence are referred to David Milner's book *Children and Race* (Penguin).

together, in a rough and ready way but systematically, a picture of children's racial attitudes in the area between the ages of four and eleven, and several heads volunteered their schools for observation or more rigorous experiments. Inevitably the picture that emerged had its lacunae, but its outlines matched almost exactly, apart from one discrepancy, those yielded by the international research evidence. Three experiments, one with nursery school children and two with top juniors, deserve to be described in some detail.

An all-white nursery school

One of the nursery school headteachers who believed that young children are innocent of racial sentiments was anxious to prove that this was so with those who attended her own school. Although the town she taught in was multiracial, the catchment area served by the school was not, so all the children were white. With the help of an educational researcher from a nearby university, who had offered the group the benefit of his expertise, she devised a simple experiment which took advantage of the fact that she taught two separate sets of children — a set who came in the morning and a set who came in the afternoon. She collected fourteen photographs, mostly taken from newspaper colour supplements, which portrayed black people in a variety of situations and in a respectful and unstereotyped way. Many of them showed black people in Britain, and one or two were multiracial. The headteacher's intention was to handle the photographs differently with the two sets of children. With the morning children she would try to stimulate discussion in her usual manner by asking questions about salient features (race and ethnicity, of course, excepted), whereas with the afternoon children she would merely draw their attention to the pictures without asking questions and so presumably encourage a freer response.

Her hypothesis was that neither in the morning nor in the afternoon would any of these white three and four year olds make reference to skin colour or comment disparagingly on what they saw. With the morning group her expectation was borne out completely. Discussion was interested and lively, but at no time did any child make reference to racial or cultural differences, even where the picture almost seemed to cry out for that kind of reaction. For instance, a photograph of a West African man wearing sunglasses and traditional dress and standing in the lounge of his London flat elicited the response, 'My daddy's got dark glasses', whilst a head and shoulders photograph of a black policeman prompted the observation, 'He's a laughing policeman.'

With the afternoon group, on the other hand, the headteacher's expectations were confounded. After three or four minutes of being shown the photographs the children began, in the words of the researcher (who observed and tape-recorded both sessions), 'to make very negative and derisory comments about the people' in them punctuated by cries of 'Ugh! Blackies!' Eventually hostility reached such a pitch that the headteacher felt obliged to intervene and close the session. Reporting back to her colleagues in the group she was quite open and undefensive about what had happened. She admitted she had been 'bowled over' by the animosity the afternoon children had displayed, and she was later to write, in answer to a questionnaire on the group's work, that the experiment 'underlined the fact that we teach on "assumptions" rather than on knowledge of what the children really think' and had changed her and her staff's ideas 'about nursery children being too young'.

The headteacher was adamant that there were no significant differences between the two groups of children. How, then, is the difference in response to the pictures to be explained? One important factor seemed to be the attitude to race she had implicitly encouraged in the school. Along with the majority of her colleagues in the teachers' group she believed not only that nursery and infant school children are unaware of race, but also that it was wrong to promote awareness by using racial or cultural labels such as 'black' and 'Pakistani' in school. In effect they sought to create a taboo on race, akin to the more familiar taboos on sex and death, which these nursery school children clearly showed signs of having learned, without ever having been directly taught, and internalized. Those present in the morning session reacted to an established classroom activity and the conventional control methodology of question and answer by behaving as they were expected to behave. They avoided the taboo subject and followed their teacher's lead in talking with warmth and interest about the pictures. To the afternoon children, on the other hand, their teacher's atypical behaviour (showing pictures without asking questions) appeared to signify a moral as well as a pedagogic withdrawal, leaving them free to respond in a relatively uninhibited fashion. Initially hostile remarks were confined to two or three children, but the rest quickly recognized what was happening and joined in the chorus of scorn. Scientifically speaking it would be impossible to substantiate this exegesis fully. Yet it does seem to match the facts of what took place and, more generally, what is known of life in classrooms.

National and cultural preference in ten and eleven year olds

Another member of the group, the headteacher of a primary school in a town further north with a small Pakistani community, asked a class of top juniors, all of whom were white, to play the balloon game. At first he invited them to imagine they were in a balloon, which they could pilot to a country of their choice, and to write the story of their journey. A week later he returned and told the class that in fact he had misinformed them and the balloon had gone out of control, ending up in a country they would rather not have visited. Once again they had to write about their experiences. The head received seventy scripts in all, two stories from each child in a class of thirty-five. The way they wrote about their two destinations can be categorized as follows:

Likes: Europe 16: Spain (6), Switzerland (4), Russia, Czechoslovakia, West Germany, Iceland, Italy, France (all 1 each)
Dominant European Culture 13; Australia (9), U.S.A. (3), Canada (1), Third World 6: Africa (3), India (2), China (1)
Dislikes: Third World 23: Africa General (5), African Countries (7), India (3), Japan (2), South America (2), Pakistan, West Indies, China, Cambodia (all 1 each)
Europe 8: Northern Ireland (5), Finalnd, England and Iceland (all 1 each)
Unclassified 4: Turkey (2), Greenland (2)

Within the first batch of stories the children who wanted to go to Europe, and to countries classified above as having 'dominant European cultures', had tourism or visits to friends and relatives in mind. The three wanting to visit Africa, and in one case it was South Africa, were more interested in hunting or viewing animals than people. African people appeared in only one story and in much the same role as they were to play in the second part of the game. 'People came running at me with spears', wrote one child causing him to fire his revolver in the air to frighten them off, but eventually he managed to 'settle down with the natives' and continue with his hunting.

In the overwhelming rejection of the Third World in the second batch of stories it was Africa and a rather generalized notion of black people living in huts in jungles who came off worst. Two images dominated the stories. One was of an inhospitable environment vitiated by poverty and disease (the Oxfam image):

'there were so many poor people that I couldn't bear to face it (India)

there is dark people they get illnesses and we might as well (Africa)

I did not like the country because of all the poor and starving people and children (Ethiopia)

everybody is hungry because they have not had any food for weeks and I would not like to see them dying round me (Africa)

It would be horrible to see them all the skinny people (Africa)'

The other image was of hostile 'natives' brandishing spears, tying up white men, and talking unintelligibly (the Tarzan image):

'we saw a bunch of nig-nogs ... then we met a chief who said 'ugapoga kono' (Africa)

thousands of black people came running talking gibberish ... grabbed hold of us. With spears at our backs we walked to their village and got thrown to the floor (Africa)

All the natives came. I was scared. They had spears. They all gathered round me. They took me to a camp ... They wore a bit of cloth for their pants ... it was the worst place I have seen in my whole life. They did not have any toilets (Africa)'

Although most pronounced in stories with African settings, the Tarzan image appeared also in the one West Indian story:

'all around us were natives. They had paint on their faces and they looked very fierce.'

And in other parts of the world too. A child visiting India 'got caught by a tribe and they would not let us go', whilst another who landed in Pakistan was confronted by two 'black women ... jabbering at one another' but saved by a 'white lady' with whom he was able to stay until his balloon was mended.

The findings of this small experiment are not perhaps particularly surprising, and certainly when they were reported to the next meeting of the headteachers' group there was a general feeling that they might have been predicted in view of the influence of the media on top junior children. Several headteachers of multiracial junior schools, however, demurred, arguing (as had the heads of multiracial nurseries in regard to the first experiment) that the beneficial effects of interracial contact in their schools would guarantee less stereotyped and hostile responses.

One of them replicated the game with a vertically grouped class of nine to eleven year olds which included a small number of

Pakistanis. As it turned out the patterns of preference and rejection evinced by the white children were almost identical to those in the all-white class already quoted. The Oxfam and Tarzan images were just as prominent in the second batch of stories, and they were joined by some unflattering portraits of Pakistan:

'I do not like their kind of food,... I do not like their clothes ... I don't think that the people would be too friendly ... we would not know what they were saying. Also I think that it would smell because of all the things they use in their food.

It smells ... They are brown. They wear a piece of cloth around them and some Pakistanis wear clothes like us. Some got to move out of Pakistan and go to England to live and some Pakistanis smell of curry. They eat horrible food. They have huts for their houses ... they have no beds to sleep on and no cars or buses or lorries.'

Equally noteworthy was the wish on the part of the Pakistani children, expressed in the first batch of stories, to return to Pakistan — a desire which seemed to be due almost as much to a sense of being rejected in England as to fond memories of their countries of origin:

'I would like to land in Pakistan because it is hot and because there is a lot of people to talk to in Pakistan and then I will go to the mosque and because everybody will come to my house and eat dinner ... I like England as well. But all the people don't like us, so I would stay in Pakistan because it is better and in Pakistan we are all brothers and sisters because God said that and it says in the Bible.'

'there is no fighting like with boys in England ... we are all brothers and sisters. That's why we do not fight. If white boys go go our church and read, they will be brothers with us. We eat and drink like other people. I do not want to go in England because I go to a school where no one likes us.'

This sense of rejection was confirmed by a taped discussion the headteacher had with a group of ten and eleven year old Indians and Pakistanis. During the course of it she asked them whether there was anything they disliked about living in England. They were unanimous that they disliked being called names — 'call me wog and black Sambo' — but what also emerged was that they gave as good as they got — 'Miss, I say white Sambos', 'I say piss off', 'I call them pink pigs' — and that their pride in being brown, Muslim and Pakistani (or, alternatively, brown, Sikh and Indian) remained unshaken — 'they're jealous' because we're brown. We're lucky.' It was in this respect that the evidence gathered by the headteachers' group was at odds with the international evidence, or at any rate with the American and British literature studying the damaging effects of low caste status on young black children. These Asian youngsters (and their attitudes seemed to be representative) manifested none of the symptoms of self-denial or identity conflict reported there. On the contrary they were full of self-confidence. The firm cultural support provided by their local community had seen to that.

Attitudes of white ten and eleven year olds to racial minorities

One of the criticisms of the original balloon game in the headteachers' group had been that it was unreal and said nothing about the children's feelings towards growing up in multiracial Britain. The headteacher concerned took the point and devised a follow-up experiment of his own to rectify the omission. He returned to the same class and showed them the CRC film strip on the Asian communities in Yorkshire, *East Comes West*, which includes sections on culture and religion, Asian children in Britain and the variety of occupations taken up by their parents. Its intentions are patently to dispel ignorance and erode stereotypes. Each frame was discussed with the children, and the headteacher commented that they 'showed great interest and readiness to contribute'.

The next day he distributed to the class copies of photographs taken in Southall. These showed the Sikh community in everyday contexts — in school, at home, in the temple, in shops and on the street. After allowing the children some time to discuss them in small groups, the headteacher asked them to write down their thoughts and feelings arising out of the film strip and the photographs 'indicating their appreciation of any particular picture as well as their own view on the problems faced by the Asian communities in our cities'.

The overall impression conveyed by the thirty-five essays was of confusion — fact commingled with error, prejudice commingled with tolerance. Consider, for example, this extract from one of them:

'I think that Pakistanis have as much right as we do but this does not happen. We think of Pakistanis as black germy people. This is not true. They have funny spots, but not germy, but if they were in their own country many would die of an illness and some would die in the war ... I think they came to be safe and have money and a proper home and family.... I don't think they should be sent back to their own country. At some time it must be stopped or England will be crowded. Already there are 55 million immigrants in England and Britain.'

Typical about this piece was the tension it articulated between feelings of benevolence and egalitarianism on the one hand and stereotypes and prejudices on the other. Attitudinal paradox — the coexistence in one individual's utterances of seemingly incompatible positions of rejection and acceptance — has been widely reported in race relations research, and we have all known children who found nothing odd in having black best friends and believing blacks as a group should be repatriated. Many of the essays seemed to be manifestations of just this syndrome, putting one in mind of Gordon Allport's famous remark about the 'peculiar double-think appropriate to prejudice in a democracy'. On the one hand the children had been socialized into stereotypes and prejudices about the Third World and British racial minorities; on the other hand they had been socialized into democratic notions of fair play and equal rights. Several of these ten and eleven year olds struggled to reconcile the two contradictory sets of ideas in their writing.

Also reported in the race relations literature is the tenuous connection between knowledge and attitudes. Some of the essays showed it was very possible to be well-informed about minority groups and still reject them. Two girls wrote neat, nicely expressed essays revealing they had learned a good deal about Asian customs and beliefs and come to appreciate their artistic achievements, but both concluded with repatriationist sentiments:

'I wish they would go back so it will be our country.'
'I wish these people would go back to their own place to live. It is getting too crowded nowadays.'

Repatriationist views bulked largely in the whole class. Although the issue had not figured in the discussion with the headteacher, no less than a third of the children voiced the opinion that there were far too many of 'them' in Britain and that they should go or be sent back 'where they came from'. The children appeared to have been told (but not by the headteacher) that there are 55 million people in Britain and that a certain percentage of these are 'immigrants' or 'blacks'.

Four children, one of whom has already been quoted, translated these figures into there being 55 million 'immigrants' in Britain, and one of them calculated that this was half of the population. The children's interpretation of the figures, accurate or not, was that Britain was too crowded and the increased proportion of blacks living here threatened specifically 'our' jobs and more generally 'our' control over the country. Here are a sample of their views:

'I think that it is not right for all them black people to come over and take over shops and things. When I go to town I see more black people taking over the stores than white people. I think that black people are trying to take over the country.'

'One day they may take over our country and ruin it ... some of them are very clever at some of our jobs. Maybe better than we are.'

'Some day I think that the coloured people are going to take over Britain, and the white people will disintegrate.'

'there are a lot of coloured people in England and some of them should be sent back where they came from.'

'black people should be sent back because soon the country will be full and there will not be enough room for us.'

Among all the hostile statements one stood out for its virulence:

'black people should not be allowed in England because England is meant for whites. England is nearly full of black people. They should be thrown out of England. Black people are funny at weddings. They have to walk round a Koran four times and I think it is very funny. There should only be white people and no more blacks left in England any longer. It is meant for white people only. White people invented more things than blacks so we should have England for whites only ... Blacks do some of the most queerest things you ever known. They are even putting black people on telly and whites invented it so only whites should go on the telly. It is not right to have black people on the telly even in England.'

This is not to say that the picture painted by the essays was uniformly bleak. Other children, besides showing that they had acquired considerable knowledge from the photographs and film strip and learned to value the accomplishments of Asian culture, championed, sometimes vigorously, the rights of black people in

Britain and attacked the perpetrators of prejudice and discrimination. But these responses were in line with the expectations of the headteachers' group. It was the incidence and intensity of repatriationist sentiments (a pointer, of course, to the effectiveness of racist propaganda in the vicinity) that astonished and alarmed them. The headteacher concerned was as open in his reaction as his nursery school colleague had been to her own experiment: in his questionnaire he wrote:

> 'As the result of observation and some research I became aware that prejudice did exist among the children in my school — I should have said quite firmly before my participation in the project that this was not so'.

The headteachers' exercise in information gathering[1] underscores the importance, as the comments of the nursery and junior heads involved implied, of working from knowledge rather than assumptions of what children think and feel about race. Even though the pattern of white attitudes revealed by their investigations could, in my experience, be replicated in most schools, it would be impossible for me to predict what the racial relationships would be in any new class I might meet, either on the basis of what my previous experience has been or on the basis of the kind of relationships I would like to foster (wish-fulfilment lies at the back of much motivated or selective perception of life in classrooms). A rather different set of relationships, for instance, were presented by the class of 12 and 13 year olds discussed in chapter 3.

If pattern and consistency are discernible in the development of children's racial attitudes, then so are paradox (as some of the quotations above have shown) and volatility. Although white children's attitudes have maintained a marked degree of consistency over the decade and a half I have been teaching them, the attitudes of black and Asian children have shifted strikingly in the past six or seven years. The Sikh and Muslim 10 and 11 year olds who talked with such self-confidence to their headteacher are representative of the determination and pride increasingly to be found among Asian children; the old stereotype of the meek and submissive Asian child is, happily, losing any contact with reality it may once have had.

The same applies to black children. The American research evidence gathered since 1939 and the British evidence gathered in the early 1970s pointed to the damaging effects of low caste status on young black children — identity conflict, poor self-esteem, even total self-denial — but the American ethnic rights and Black Power movements of the 60s, and their British equivalents, have secured a remarkable transformation. I do not mean that black self-rejection as a phenomenon has disappeared; far from it. Infant schools still report distressing stories of black children depicting themselves as white in self-portraits or covering themselves in white chalk or attempting to scrub the colour off their skins. While I was working in educational research, a black secretary in the office told me of how she had been watching television with her four year old son when he suddenly remarked that a man on the screen was black. His mother agreed and added that the man was like him in this respect. To her surprise her son denied his own blackness and, in response to further questioning, the blackness of his mother and of his closest relatives. Though persuaded eventually to agree that his mother and family were black, he persisted resolutely with the fiction of his own non-blackness. At about the same time I collected a piece of writing entitled 'Myself' which a black girl in her final year of junior school had written along with the rest of her class. Part of what she wrote reads:

> 'I wish that I had long hair, but I have not got long hair. I do not like myself and my writing. I do not like the colour of my eyes. I have spots on my skin which I wish that I never had ... In the future I think that I am going to turn ... black, ever so black, and ugly just like I am now, ugly.'

On the other hand, a black boy in the same class felt self-confident enough to launch into his essay with 'I am black', whilst another wrote: 'I was born in the West Indies.... My face is like my dad's and my hair. People say that I am a nice boy ... and my hair is soft and bumpy.' Increasingly black British youngsters are identifying strongly with the newly emergent black culture which sets such ostentatious store by pride in race and affirmation of ancestry. Unfortunately, far from welcoming this positive transformation in self-esteem, many schools have chosen to interpret the demonstrations and symbols of black pride and solidarity (all-black groups in the playground, the use of Creole in the classroom, and the wearing of woolly hats and the colours of Rastafarianism) as hostile forces threatening their well-being.

Of course, black youth culture is in a sense a vigorous response to bitter experiences of white racism; so it is understandable, if regrettable, that some of the manifestations of black pride (but none of those quoted above) should involve fiercely anti-white or separatist stances. To the new mood of black militancy school is almost as inimical an institution as the police, and truculence in the classroom as justifiable a form of black resistance as preferring unemployment to menial jobs. Evidence of just how bad relationships have become in some schools is furnished by a recent book on West Indian children in Britain written by a black American academic.[2] A headteacher quoted in the book recounts how she was walking along the road hand-in-hand with a five year old black boy when he said: 'My father shouldn't see me now ... walking up the road with a white woman'; and another head tells of a black seven year old who, on being reprimanded by his teacher, called her a 'white racist pig.' At one secondary school 'a state of warfare' is said to exist between the staff and the black students; and at another a black studies teacher describes how black students objected to whites joining the class — 'Get de raas outside here, mon, dis de black man ting.' In considering these and similar incidents the author is at pains to argue, and quite rightly, that teachers should resist the temptation to concentrate 'on the symptoms of the black pupils' response to racism' to the neglect 'of the elimination of its causes.'

One of the sad consequences of this polarization in attitudes is the impossible position in which the many black children who are neither militants nor separatists are placed. I am thinking, for example, of Phyllis who was deputy head girl at my school last year. She was articulate, hard-working and vivacious; and excelled n cookery, music and sport. Popular with staff and pupils alike, she held particular sway over black children in middle and lower school. She was also prone to moments of self-doubt — even self-denial. When the black group failed to turn up for the Christmas youth club dance, she was reported to have said, 'Typical. You can't trust coloureds.' Shortly after that episode I was reading *Lord of the Flies* with half of my CSE English set. Phyllis was the only black pupil present. We came to the part where Piggy shouts at Jack's tribe, 'Which is better — to be a pack of painted niggers like you are, or to be sensible like Ralph is?' Eleven pairs of eyes turned on Phyllis, and a couple of white boys guffawed. She bridled angrily — 'just 'cause I'm the only black kid here.' At the end of the lesson I talked to her. Although she quite understood how Piggy had come to say what he did, she had been deeply upset by her white class-mates' mockery. It brought to mind all those other occasions — at school, in the street — when she had been abused for her colour.

Yet Phyllis's experience of white racism had not pushed her into militancy or separatism. She was a staunch integrationist — 'there's good and bad in all races' — and strongly criticized the anti-white stances taken up by other black youngers. Once, she told me, she had gone to this dance, only to realize when she got there that it was an all-black affair. She felt acutely embarrassed (it seemed a denial of her many white friendships) and took it out on the first boy to ask her to dance. He asked in Creole and she refused 'in Birmingham', knowing that the choice of white speech would wound more than the refusal. Similarly, a devout Christian, Phyllis felt more drawn to the Jehovah's Witnesses than the black churches which, she argued, were 'against the spirit of Christianity.'

On the other hand, she was an avid reader of the black books in the school library, being especially excited by Linton Kwesi Johnson's collection of dialect poems *Dream, Beat and Blood* (Bogle L'Ouverture), and organized and directed a dialect play (a rehearsal of which I was watching one evening when the school caretaker came up and whispered in my ear, 'What's this all about? Witchdoctors?') For a career Phyllis's first choice was the police, but family and community persuaded her that this was not quite appropriate for a black girl. She then set her sights on teaching home economics (she would make an admirable teacher), but at her interview for further education college it was suggested that nursing might be a better idea.

Obviously this portrait is partial and subjective, since it is based on one white teacher's selected perceptions. But it can, I believe, claim a certain representativeness; and it illustrates both the range of pressures bearing on black children and the danger of deducing anything definitive about a child's attitudes from isolated reactions or utterances. Consider, for example, the case of Diana, a third year girl of Indian and Irish parentage (mixed race children are perhaps the most vulnerable of all). After watching a television programme on adoption, which included the information that black and mixed race children were two categories where children for adoption exceeded prospective adopters, she wrote, 'I would not adopt a child of a different race because if the child was black when it was older it might not like having a white mum or dad.' A mature observation, but seemingly also a straightforward denial on Diana's part of her Indianness — understandable enough, because her parents had separated and she lived with her Irish mother. Yet during an informal lunchtime conversation between Diana, myself and her two closest friends (one black, one white) the black girl said that black people call themselves 'beef', white people 'pork' and half castes 'mutton', to which Diana promptly responded with, 'Well, I'm mutton then.' The most enigmatic of all utterances are the racial jokes which are such a constant feature of classrooms and playgrounds in multi-racial schools. The same black girl greeted my request to give some books out (without being quite sure of how serious or funny she was trying to be) with, 'I may be black, but I'm not a slave.' On another occasion a third year Pakistani boy allowed me to jump ahead of him in the dinner queue and his white friend quipped, 'He may be a Bangladesh, but he's a gentleman.' How such jests are to be interpreted and what importance should be attached to them are issues I return to in a later chapter when discussing pupils' reactions to the introduction of multiracial materials.

The headteachers' exercise in information gathering is indicative of the sort of openness to pupils' thoughts and experiences and the sort of analysis which should be integral to curriculum planning. It would be nonsense to purport to plan a multiracial curriculum without first taking stock of the racial ideas and feelings children unquestionably have. Those evident in the written and oral responses cited in this chapter are extremely suggestive of the curriculum objectives and content teachers should be addressing themselves to.

Race is, of course, a delicate area; children's sensitivities are at stake. It goes without saying that gathering information about it demands more than ordinary tact and discretion. The replication, for instance, of the first experiment in a multiracial nursery school would be inconceivable. But there are no grounds for arguing, as some critics of investigating children's racial attitudes do, that the whole enterprise is irresponsible and should never be attempted. The only irresponsibility would lie in taking no curriculum action once the information had been gathered.

References

1 I should like to acknowledge my indebtedness to the three head-teachers most closely involved for their cooperation, and to Jill Baldwin and Eric O'Hare for their assistance in collecting the data.
2 Raymond Giles *The West Indian Experience in British Schools* (Heinemann).

2 The Idea of a Multiracial Curriculum

'by far the most important question that can be raised about education is the question what to teach.'
Mary Warnock

'Rational curriculum planning must take account of the realities of classroom situations. It is not enough to be logical.'
Lawrence Stenhouse

The idea of a multiracial curriculum is deceptively simple. It can be defined as a curriculum whose choice of content reflects the multi-racialness of Britain and the world and draws significantly on the experiences of British racial minorities and cultures overseas. The development of such a curriculum can be justified in a number of different ways.

The most elaborate constitutes what I have called elsewhere the 'pathological' foundation for developing a multiracial curriculum — 'pathological', because it is premised on the assumption that British society suffers from an endemic malaise, racism, which has acquired the status of a cultural norm and moulds children's attitudes to the extent illustrated in the previous chapter. Because its influence is so pervasive and pernicious, the argument runs, schools have a clear duty to ensure that they utilize the eleven years children spend compulsorily under their aegis to make a concerted response by promoting racial self-respect and interracial under-standing. The second justification is based on the notion of minority group rights and says, in effect, that racial minorities are entitled to expect that their cultures will be prominently and positively represented in the school curriculum. In the United States this notion is enshrined in federal and state legislation, but in this country, perhaps because the debate about race has been confound-ed with the debate about immigration, it has yet to secure a firm purchase. The third justification rests on the traditional view that one of the school's tasks is to present its pupils with an accurate picture of the society, and world, in which they are growing up; unquestionably other races and cultures are important elements in that picture. The final justification, not *prima facie* perhaps the most compelling, simply claims that a curriculum which is multi-racial involves pupils in more stimulating, interesting and challeng-ing learning experiences than one which is not.

Against these justifications can be set four grounds for resisting the development of a multiracial curriculum which are commonly put forward. Two of these — the insignificance of race to young children and the unacceptably 'political' cast to such a curriculum — I have attempted to deal with already. The other two receive direct or indirect comment later in this chapter. The first is the straightforward ideological contention that the business of British schools, however composed, is to transmit British culture to each new generation. The second maintains that multiracial innovations in the curriculum have too often been shown to yield counter-productive effects.

Had I to offer some account or defence of my own current curriculum practice, I should choose to do so on the basis of a combination of justifications two, three and four. It is not that I no longer accept the analysis inherent in the first justification; it will be apparent from the introduction and from my interpretation of the research and observation described in the previous chapter that I accept it totally. But as a justification it is open to several serious reservations. First, if the ultimate aim is to persuade more schools and teachers of the need for instituting multiracial policies for curriculum and organisation, it is too tendentious; secondly, it runs the risk of implying that schools which could fairly lay claim to good race relations would have no reason for instituting such policies; and, thirdly, it is inclined to result in heavily authoritarian teaching.

Nevertheless, it was with the 'pathological' justification that my own thinking about the multiracial curriculum began, and I should like to embark on marking out my present position by referring to an article 'Curriculum planning in multiracial education' I wrote three years ago which bears the justification's imprint. In it a strongly expressed concern for the evolution of a more equitable multiracial society led me to ascribe primacy in the development of a multiracial curriculum to a delineation of objectives and the rehabilitation of content. I identified the opposition as the ideology of child-centred progressivism which seemed to me to dominate the theory, if not always the practice, of education between the years of 5 and 13. My reading of the ideology was that it confined the delineation of objectives to skills and conceptual understandings and subordinated curriculum content, 'mere facts', to classroom processes and learning methodologies. The reasoning behind these two emphases I traced to the ideology's overall aim that children should become autonomous — equipped to control their own learning and master their own destinies. Over affective objectives I found the ideology tentative and even ambivalent; quick to agree that schools have responsibility for children's moral and emotional development but reluctant to translate this recognition into curriculum objectives or content, insisting instead that what schools can do is best done by example or indirectly through the tacit lessons of their ethos.

In taking issue with child-centredness on objectives I borrowed from the American educationalist Eliot Eisner his useful distinction between 'instructional' and 'expressive' objectives. Broadly speaking this distinction corresponds to the distinction made in Bloom and Krathwohl's taxonomy of objectives between cognitive and affective domains. In the cognitive domain of knowledge and skills there will generally be identifiable objectives that can be pre-specified and teachers, in view of their more complete mastery of that knowledge and those skills, will naturally expect to have overriding authority for deciding what the objectives are to be. In the affective or 'expressive' domain, on the other hand, or rather in those sections of it where there are no simple or correct outcomes and where the ultimate targets are to do with creativity or forming one's own opinions and conclusions, only the learning situation can be pre-specified; the outcomes will be various and arise out of negotiation between teacher and learner.

Whilst conceding the need for flexibility in deciding on objectives — to allow for unintended outcomes and for the objectives of pupils and parents — I concluded that the development of a multiracial curriculum requires pre-specified instructional objectives rather than expressive objectives restricted to descriptions of educational encounters*, because fundamental to such a curriculum is the assumption that the purpose of schooling is to bring about desired changes in children which, once identified and specified, should therefore serve as the starting point and focus for curriculum planning. Moreover, although these changes would be primarily to do with attitudes and dispositions, they represent a different sort of affectivity from the affectivity of creative work and aesthetic judgement. They are necessary for children and for society, I argued; they could not be said to be open to negotiation, nor can they be left to chance. I tabulated them in the form of a Bloomian taxonomy of objectives divided into two broad affective categories

---

*Lawrence Stenhouse is right to criticise Eisner for continuing to refer to these descriptions as 'objectives'.

—respect for others and respect for self. Under these headings I listed some twenty objectives — skills, knowledge, attitudes — which I characterized as necessary for the achievement of the ultimate goals of interracial respect and racial self-respect.

Where, then, do I stand now on this somewhat tortuous but by no means wholly academic dispute? It is natural, even inevitable, that a shift in viewpoint should accompany moving from curriculum research and development to classroom teaching. The teacher, after all, has to be constantly (and often instantaneously) active and decisive in a way alien to the researcher's experience. So it is hardly surprising that teachers and researchers should differ so regularly over defining problems and isolating issues. The previous chapter provided examples of teachers of young children defying the evidence of research and misreading their pupils' thoughts and feelings about race. But it is not a monopoly of teachers to get things wrong. Sometimes the views to be found among the class-room outsiders (lecturers, advisers, community workers and so forth) who make up the multiracial education lobby (I intend no slur by this label) appear to be distinctly skewed.

It did not take many weeks back in the classroom, after an absence of four years, for me to discover (perhaps I had just forgotten) that I was a child-centred progressivist. There was no other way I wanted to work with my pupils; which meant I had to rethink that part of the article's argument which I have summarised above. It will come as no surprise to critics of the objectives school of 'rational curriculum planning' that eighteen months had elapsed before I felt disposed or able to attempt an itemization of object-ives. Prior to that my classroom initiatives had been exploratory and experimental; indeed they still essentially are. Although there is clearly a place for the specification of objectives in English teaching, notably in the area of literacy skills, most of what goes on is 'expressive' rather than 'instructional'. When I came to the task (the result can be found in chapter 4), not only did I want to attach overriding importance to skills and concepts (and, as above, in the interests of children becoming autonomous), but also I wanted very much to disown affective goals such as respect for self and others. The curriculum model I proposed in the article now strikes me as too prescriptive and too moralistic.

Those teachers who feel tentative or ambivalent about objectives in the affective domain are reacting to sound instincts. There are substantial dangers (indoctrination, counterproductive effects, for instance) in schools annexing territory — children's attitudes —

which is not by common consent properly theirs. At the time of writing the article it was not uncommon to be told by representatives of minority communities that the self-image of black and brown children was no business of the schools and that it was arrogant and presumptuous of them ever to have imagined it might be. It is equally arrogant and presumptuous, I would now say, for schools to stipulate as a curriculum target that children should respect other races and cultures. Implicitly it is to treat children as objects who need something doing to them. Children's attitudes and opinions are their own affair; by which I do not mean that no place should be found in school for them to be discussed and explored, but that in the last analysis it is for children to determine what they should be.

Furthermore, curriculum objectives should be arrived at following consultation with pupils and parents. The structure to make such consultation possible scarcely exists. Indeed its establishment would be fiercely resisted by many teachers and their unions. But at the very least teachers could make their objectives explicit to the recipients and consumers. Certainly I try to. It is hard to envisage telling one's pupils that two of one's objectives were racial self-respect and interracial respect. There is something almost necessarily secretive about such goals. Were they to be made public, many pupils and parents would, for a variety of reasons, find them anathema.

I trust it will not be thought that I do not want my pupils to respect themselves and others. Obviously I do. But that is a hope, not a curriculum objective. There is a genuine difficulty here over distinguishing between a concern for children's moral welfare and being moralistic. Educational theorists and curriculum writers have long recognised the relationship between a school's choice of curriculum and its philosophy of life. 'The objectives to be finally included,' write the authors of the Bloomian taxonomy, 'should be related to the school's view of the "good life for the individual in good society" ';[2] or, as Mary Warnock puts it, 'the determining of the school curriculum is the most crucial evaluation that has to be made, and ... it has to be made on the criterion of contribution to the good life.'[3] Similarly, schools have always accepted responsibility, some at any rate, for the behaviour of the pupils in their care. But behaviour is not the same thing as attitudes; and, in any case, children no more learn morality from being the targets of attitudinal objectives than they do from morning assembly homilies. They learn from examples and models — in this case from the examples and models provided by the school and its staff; above all from the way their teachers behave towards them as individuals with rights as well as needs.

Here I would like to draw together some conclusions:

1 Much of what is undertaken by schools is not conducive to 'operationalization' as curriculum objectives. It is tentative, exploratory, hypothetical — and rightly so. It is not because, as some American behaviourists insist, teachers do not know what they are doing; but because that is the way of life in classrooms. Although what Eliot Eisner calls 'expressive' objectives (i.e. descriptions of classroom encounters and not objectives at all) are particularly appropriate in the humanities and the expressive arts, they may have relevance elsewhere too.

2 Child-centred progressivism is right to ascribe curriculum primacy to the aim that children should become autonomous — controllers of their own learning and masters of their own destinies — and to confine objectives, by and large, to necessary skills and conceptual understandings. It is also right to set store by classroom processes and learning methodologies.

3 Some affective objectives have a place in the curriculum — for instance, those to do with aesthetic appreciation and attitudes towards work and learning — but others, specifically those stipulating which moral attitudes and opinions are to be promoted, do not.

4 Most knowledge objectives are unnecessary. They can be more simply and traditionally presented as curriculum content.*

From these conclusions it will be apparent that I now believe the child-centred ideology, notwithstanding the excesses of some of its exponents, to be a good deal more right about the curriculum than wrong, and partly at least — which may come as a surprise to its critics — because it is grounded in classroom realities.

However, excesses there indubitably have been, and I should like to turn to one in particular, the depreciation of the value of curriculum content, because of its special relevance for multiracial education. Some exponents of child-centredness have certainly seemed to imply not only that content is less important than process

*But note the importance I attach to one knowledge objective in English teaching in chapter 4.

and method, but also that it is merely instrumental to the attainment of overall skills and concepts and that, therefore, provided those targets are reached it almost does not matter what content is chosen. So, for instance, as long as children succeed in developing the necessary historical skills (sifting evidence, forming hypotheses, and so on), it is neither here nor there whether they have fashioned them on the study of the French Revolution or on the study of the British brewing industry. Without wishing to detract from the importance accorded skills and concepts, I want to insist that the choice of content is of paramount importance (hence the epigraph from Mary Warnock which heads this chapter), because one of the purposes of schooling (justification three above) is to engage children with an accurate picture of the world, both its past and its present, in which they are growing up. Naturally there will be disagreement, considerable and acrimonious maybe, about what constitutes an 'accurate picture', but the attempt has to be made.

At the outset of this discussion I defined a multiracial curriculum exclusively in terms of its content. What distinguishes it are the facts, themes and ideas which make it up and the materials deployed to service them. Given this emphasis, content choice becomes crucial; in the article to which I have referred I listed five fundamental criteria for the selection of learning experiences for a multiracial curriculum. They are reproduced below. What they amount to is a reasonably specific set of prescriptions and proscriptions relating to the quality and quantity of presentation of the experiences and accomplishments of other races and cultures.

*Criteria for the selection of learning experiences for a multiracial curriculum**

1 An insular curriculum, preoccupied with Britain and British values, is unjustifiable in the final quarter of the twentieth century. The curriculum needs to be both international in its choice of content and global in its perspective.

*There is no contradiction involved in arguing both for 'expressive' objectives in the attitudinal area of the affective domain and for prescriptive criteria for content choice, since the purpose of the latter is simply to make available a more accurate picture of the world. I should add that I would see criteria of this order being arrived at voluntarily by teachers. I am not one of those who believe in the imposition of mandatory criteria (on the American model) by legislation, the DES or the LEAs.

2 Contemporary British society contains a variety of social and ethnic groups; this variety should be made evident in the visuals, stories and information offered to children.

3 Pupils should have access to accurate information about racial and cultural differences and similarities.

4 People from British minority groups and from other cultures overseas should be presented as individuals with every variety of human quality and attribute. Stereotypes of minority groups in Britain and of cultures overseas, whether expressed in terms of human characteristics, life-styles, social roles or occupational status, are unacceptablé and likely to be damaging.

5 Other cultures and nations have their own validity and should be described in their own terms. Wherever possible they should be allowed to speak for themselves and not be judged exclusively against British or European norms.

Obviously it is more than just a matter of increasing the visibility of the black experience in the curriculum. It has also to be ensured that the manner of its presentation, to borrow the epithets of justification two above, is both 'prominent and positive'; that is to say, extensive and accurate, unstereotyped and varied. What the criteria do not do, however, is to stipulate the curriculum form or shape the incorporation of minority experience is to take; and decisions about curriculum form, and indeed substance, are particularly germane to the final ground for resisting multiracial innovations I quoted which says that they are highly prone to counter-productive effects. Many schools and teachers have discovered that innovations of an overtly multiracial kind (units on the Caribbean, topics on Diwali or slavery) are often poorly received — by black children as well as white. There are a number of reasons for this.

If the curriculum norm is white and European, minority children may well be embarrassed at being placed so conspicuously in the limelight by a sudden intrusion from their own culture. Whilst white children may (and frequently do) react hostilely, interpreting the teacher's decision as partisan and further confirmation of a more general black takeover of the school, the neighbourhood and the country. Sometimes minority children's embarrassment has been exacerbated and their white peers' hostility converted to scorn by unbalanced or inadvisable selections of content from the cultures of countries and continents of immigrant origin. I am thinking, for example, of teaching about the Indian subcontinent which leans almost entirely on the British aid agencies for its materials or teaching about the transatlantic slave trade which, like the unit described in the next chapter, fails to give either black or white children enough to identify with or feel positive about. Such negative reactions are obviously more likely in schools where race relations are bad; they are also less likely, or so I would hypothesize, where the multiracial principle I spoke of in the introduction has been firmly established in the curriculum — where, in other words, the experience of minority cultures and the presence of black and brown people are perfectly normal features of children's everyday learning.

On the Schools Council project we came to several conclusions about teaching humanities in the middle school years which are pertinent to the present discussion.*

1 Generally speaking there is very little to be said for isolated topics on India, Africa or the Caribbean which are not part of a comprehensive multiracial curriculum policy. Not only are they liable to counterproductive effects, especially in schools with poor race relations, but also by their very nature they can only make occasional curriculum appearances.

2 A sounder approach, in terms of curriculum tactics, is to construct a learning programme around regular themes which draw on a variety of cultures for source material and with which all children can, therefore, identify. So, to take an obvious example, in religious education, a syllabus founded on themes to which all faiths can contribute — sacrifice, worship, pilgrimage, and so forth — is preferable to one which allocates Judaism, Christianity, Islam, Hinduism, Sikhism and Buddhism a term each. This approach both reduces the chances of counterproductive effects, since no child could reasonably claim it was partisan, and satisfies the basic multiracial principle of making minority experience a fixed feature of the curriculum.

3 Nevertheless, the need for some kind of overt systematic study remains, since themes cannot of themselves provide children with an appreciative understanding of the logic and integrity of a way of life different to their own. This level of understanding is perhaps

---

*I have rephrased some of these conclusions. They can be found in their original form, together with the discussion that led to them, in the as yet unpublished Project report, *Multiracial Education : Curriculum and Context 5 — 13*, chapters 9 and 10.

most easily achieved through the overt study of a culture unrepresented in the school's pupil population, for by being in a sense 'neutral' it will not strike children as partisan nor have to contend with deeply entrenched hostile attitudes. Once achieved, such understanding can be utilized in making a more direct approach, in the early years of secondary school, say, to the cultures of British minorities.

4 The humanities curriculum in the middle years of schooling should divide its attention evenly between local and international studies which, in addition, should complement one another in the process whereby a child makes sense of his or her world. It is particularly important that schools, having taken the decision to incorporate minority cultures in their curricula, should not define those cultures exclusively in terms of patterns of life and experience in countries and continents of origin. Children may well find more that is immediately meaningful in the new, evolving forms of minority culture taking shape in Britain.

5 The type of investigation of the Third World usually known as development studies, popular with some secondary schools, too often infringes the fifth criterion above by making European concepts and categories integral to its operations. However, it involves necessary knowledge, and there is no sense in which its objectives and multiracial objectives are incompatible. A synthesis needs to be forged between them.[4]

This last conclusion, and indeed the fifth criterion above, can serve as reminders that a multiracial curriculum involves a change in perspective as well as a change in content — an end, in effect, to ethnocentricism which does not so much exclude other cultures as view them in a disparaging or, at best, condescending light. The fifth criterion can also serve to introduce the final stage in this chapter's discussion which has to do with the relationship between content and method and between curriculum and culture.

A curriculum represents a selection from the cultural skills, phenomena and experiences available to it. A multiracial curriculum is one whose selection draws on cultures with overseas origins as well as on indigenous sources. This might appear to be to limit curriculum to content, even to make it synonymous with content; but defining a multiracial curriculum in terms of content is neither to deny the crucial significance rightly ascribed by the child-centred ideology to classroom processes and learning methodologies, nor is it to dodge the complicated issues surrounding the school's perception of its function in regard to the cultural content it embodies in the curriculum and the communities it is supposed to serve.

In my article of three years ago I referred to the longstanding debate as to whether the school's function is to transmit or transform culture.* Traditionally all societies have sought to transmit their cultures to the next generation, whether through formal or informal educational processes, and there are those who, albeit defining 'culture' more narrowly, would continue to see this as the school's main purpose today. But there is clearly a difference between a 'simple' society which can still boast of a discrete common culture — an agreed set of rituals, beliefs and values — to pass on to its young; and contemporary Britain fragmented and diversified culturally by industrialisation and urbanisation and which, even when discounting for the moment the cultures of recently arrived ethnic minorities, incorporates a great variety of rituals, beliefs and values.

Modern transmissionists argue that, notwithstanding the bewildering multiplicity of knowledge and diversity of beliefs available to curriculum planners, it is still possible and indeed desirable, to sift out what Matthew Arnold called 'the best that has been known and thought in the world'. Schools are conceived of by this view as passing on to the next generation a cultural heritage defined by criteria of intellectual excellence.

Critics of the view have maintained that too often this heritage has merely represented the fossilized formulations of the values and interests of the middle class and that the curriculum ought to draw equally on the various social and regional subcultures making up our plural society which have up to now been discounted and devalued. It is a simple extension to this criticism to maintain, in the manner of justification two above, that the cultures of recently established ethnic minorities also have an entitlement to curriculum inclusion. I certainly believe that the curriculum should constitute the school's attempt to sift out 'the best that has been known and thought in the world', intractable as the task may prove, but an

---

*The distinction made here between 'transmissionist' and 'transformationist' views of the relationship between school and culture can be compared with Paulo Freire's distinction between 'banking' and 'problemposing' education and Douglas Barnes's distinction between teaching as 'transmission' and teaching as 'interpretation'.

attempt which would not be open to the charge of being narrowly middle-class or ethnocentric. I do not believe, however, that it is the school's function to 'transmit' a curriculum so constituted, for central to that concept seems to be the idea of teaching as instruction and learning as passive reception.

The alternative transformationist view is that if a new viable common culture is to emerge, what has previously passed for the 'cultural heritage' requires to be opened up to critical revaluation, and indeed that future cultural resilience will demand that critical revaluation becomes an established feature of our society. The school's function will be to involve its pupils in just this process, and here it is possible to relate the transformationist view to child-centredness. For schools to participate significantly in the process of cultural revaluation they will need to attach primacy to the development of those same overall skills which the child-centred ideology takes to be indispensable to children becoming autonomous. If one of the school's aims should be to present pupils with its version of 'the best that has been known and thought in the world', then another should be to ensure that they leave school equipped with their own — or rather, equipped with the ability to formulate their own, to decide for themselves which knowledge, in Herbert Spencer's famous phrase, is of most worth.

Transformationism (in the notion that the school should aspire to the status of social critic and cultural synthesizer) involves the multiracial school in particular difficulty. For it does not serve one society or culture or even a collection of related sub-groups and sub-cultures. It serves several quite separate and sometimes markedly diverse cultures whose beliefs and values may well not only differ but actually conflict. It is hard to imagine how the school could hope to serve such diverse cultures in quite the same way. It is, after all, not a value-free institution; nor could it ever be, no matter how 'open' its relationship with the surrounding community. Not only does it serve a society and a culture or cultures; it *is* itself a society and a culture with identifiable values and rituals to which its members are expected to conform.

It has been argued in the past that there is a discontinuity between the culture of the school and the culture of the working class child, and that, because the culture of the school is to all intents and purposes synonymous with the culture of the dominant middle class, implicit in this discontinuity will be the disparagement of everything — language, expectations, behaviour — the working class child brings to school with him. It is now being argued that minority race children are in a similar, only more acute, position. Their culture too is likely to be ignored, under-estimated or disparaged by the school. The purpose of a multiracial curriculum is to rectify these omissions, imbalances and inequities. But it is extremely unlikely that a multiracial curriculum in a transformationist school will rectify them in a manner entirely acceptable to many representatives of the racial minorities them-selves, simply because they will not share the school's view that all children have an inalienable right to choose their own career and determine their own beliefs, values and way of life.

Consider, for example, the case of Muslim children in Britain. Many of them attend Quran schools in the evening where they are taught the tenets of Islam, the life of Mohamed and Muslim ethics as matters of fact and faith; they will not be encouraged to regard what they have been told critically. During the day at school, on the other hand, they may well find themselves in quite different learning atmospheres where the emphasis is not on their learning facts or items of faith but on being creative and critical, on forming their own opinions and making their own decisions. In other words, they may be in the perplexing position of attending a school in the day time which interprets the school's function as transformationist and one in the evening which interprets its function as transmission-ist. Part at any rate of the motivation behind Muslim pressure for their own schools is that they fear the effects of child-centred education on their children. What has to be said quite emphati-cally, so far as maintained schools are concerned, is that, whilst racial minorities are entitled to demand that their cultures be represented prominently and positively, they are not entitled to demand that they be represented uncritically. It is not the business of the maintained schools to turn out good Muslims any more than it is their business to turn out good Christians, Jews or Sikhs.

It is reassuring to find this view echoed by an Asian educational-ist.[5] Criticising the philosophy of 'ethnic reinforcement', A.S. Abrahams wrote:

'learning about one's culture to establish identity and self-pride is one thing, learning about it so that it impedes acculturation in a modern, egalitarian, technological society is another.'

The preservation of minority cultures in a fossilized form is not what multiracial schools should be doing, he went on; instead their aim for minority group pupils should be to make them 'critically aware of their culture and equipped to decide themselves how much to retain', which is precisely the sort of aim child-centred transformationism might come up with. Some minority children will choose to adapt fairly closely to British norms; others will choose to retain customs and beliefs almost identical to those they or their parents or their grandparents knew in their countries of origin; and there will be all kinds of other possibilities in between. The school's duty is to ensure that its philosophy, policies, curricula and so on are such as to enable and accommodate as many choices as are feasible. The bounds of feasibility will be marked out by the values the school believes to be integral to its own culture, to its concept of the good life; and there is no escaping the fact that the child-centred transformationist British school will, if only implicitly, be pushing its pupils in certain directions rather than others and that these may well prove unpopular with sections of the minority communities (to say nothing of the white majority).

It can readily be deduced from what I have said in this chapter why I now believe that the child-centred ideology to be correct in attaching such importance to classroom processes and learning methodologies.* In the first place, if pupils are to be meaningfully engaged with the school's curriculum, with its definition of 'the best that has been thought and known in the world', they must be able to make it properly their own — to relate it to what they already know and have experienced; the achievement of this will depend upon the institution of open patterns of communication and language use in the classroom. Secondly, if they are to leave school autonomous (which includes, of course, a capacity for social commitment and resourcefulness as well as a capacity for independent thought and action) — equipped, that is, to determine their own cultural allegiance and to participate in their generation's remaking of the cultural heritage — then, they are going to have to develop a whole range of skills and understandings which can only really be fashioned and refined by the regular experience of problem-posing styles of learning.

---

*It took a stimulating and incisive article by Alan James to bring me round: 'Why Language Matters', *Multiracial School,* Summer 1977. What he has to say about language, and the inseparability of content and method, can be seen as a translation of the ideas of Douglas Barnes (and others) to the multiracial classroom.

References

1 'Curriculum planning in multiracial education' *Educational Research* June 1976
2 Bloom B. et al. *Taxonomy of Educational Objectives* — Handbook I (Longman 1956) p 27
3 Mary Warnock *Schools of Thought* (Faber) p 168
4 This point is taken up at length by Mary Worrall in 'Multiracial Britain and the Third World — tensions and approaches in the classroom' *The New Era* March/April 1978.
5 A.S. Abrahams 'Time to help the underdog' *Times Educational Supplement* 27th September 1974.

3 A Multiracial Classroom Observed

'It seems to me that the style and quality of communication in classrooms may do more good or harm to children's attitudes than any of the curriculum content, images or stereotypes to which they are exposed.'
Alan James

The study which forms the basis of this chapter was originally conceived as an exercise in curriculum assessment. It set out to monitor the impact of a half-term unit on the Caribbean (part of a two years integrated humanities curriculum) on a second year class in a multiracial inner-city comprehensive school. At the time (it was late in 1975) I was working on the Schools Council project, and one of my particular interests lay in taking a close look at innovations of an overtly multiracial kind (topics on India and Africa, for example) in the humanities area of the middle school curriculum. I was inclined to define a curriculum's impact rather narrowly in terms of its measured effects on the racial knowledge and attitudes of the pupils experiencing it. We were concerned on the project with the tendency of overt multiracial innovations to yield counter-productive effects — alienating white pupils and discomforting blacks — and were in the process of arguing, along the lines suggested in the previous chapter, both that the best kind of innovation might not be overt and that where it was, as in teaching about countries or continents of immigrant origin, special care needed to be exerted over the selection of objectives and content.

In the event, whilst contributing to the development of this argument, the study proved to be insightful in quite other ways. It demonstrated that the realisation of a curriculum is never reducible, not even in the most traditional classroom, to its impact on pupils. The class in the study certainly did not experience their humanities course in any passive fashion. In 'enacting' it, to use Douglas Barnes's valuable term, they brought to it ideas and feelings of their own, related it to what they already knew and occasionally shifted its direction. More generally, the study highlighted the importance of the curriculum's social context to its success — the racial climate in the neighbourhood and the school, the relationship between teacher[1] and pupils and the styles of learning and patterns of communication established in the class-room.

The school involved served a downtown catchment area of new council housing and flats and condemned and derelict streets. Its eight form entry of approximately 1,000 pupils was divided for teaching purposes into two broad ability bands. Of the 40% who were of minority ethnic origin the majority were black, together with a significant number of mixed black/white parentage and a few Chinese, Indians and Pakistanis. The racial composition of the class chosen for the study, which was in the upper band of the second year, is shown below. Of the non-white children only two were themselves immigrants — Jaykishan who had come from Tanzania when he was two and Wendy who had come from Barbados two years before. The seven black children were all of Jamaican ancestry except for Wendy and Anthony who was half African. All the mixed race children had white mothers; in three cases the father was African, and in one (Christine's) he was Jamaican.

The Class

White	Black	Mixed Race
Andrew	Anthony	Christine (G)
Christine (B)	Clifton	Corinne
Donna	Dorian	Maria
Gabrielle	Gary	Max
Jacqueline	Roger	(4)
Janet	Trevor	
Joyce	Wendy	
Julie	(7)	*Indian*
Lee		Jaykishan
Paul (H)		(1)
Paul (O)		
Richard		
Robert		
Sharon		
Tina		
(15)		

The humanities course attempted to integrate English, Geography, History and Religious Education in the first two years. Its approach was basically geographical, graduating from the neighbourhood, the city and Britain in the first year to the Caribbean, Africa and the Indian sub-continent in the second, but most of its material, at any rate in the second year, was historical. The Caribbean content covered during the assessment period included Columbus, the Arawak Indians, early European settlement, the Atlantic slave trade, life on the plantations, and immigration into Britain. Much of it derived from Longman's three volume secondary school history for the Caribbean, *The People Who Came*. In addition there was a section of Caribbean books in the library to draw on, and the teacher in the study (ML) made use of Paula Fox's *The Slave Dancer* (Piccolo), Mary Cockett's *Another Home Another Country* (Chatto, Boyd and Oliver) and Julius Lester's *To Be a Slave* (Puffin).

The assessment of the unit comprised classroom observation, scrutiny of the pupils' work, the administration of a knowledge test and taped interviews with ten children. In undertaking it I was not conscious of making any major contribution to the theory of evaluation. There are educational researchers who would like to elevate curriculum evaluation (and classroom observation in particular) to quasi-scientific status — as a new branch of social anthropology, for instance. My interests were more mundane. I deliberately confined myself to the sort of obvious activities any perspicacious teacher could, and should, undertake; all they would require would be the right organisational framework (team-teaching, notably) to release their time and energies.*

Classroom observation

During the period of assessment I observed eight double lessons. I reproduce here extracts covering four of them from the notebook I kept together with discussions of some of the issues they posed.

1 The first extract is from an early lesson which introduced the class to the Caribbean through a pre-independence filmstrip entitled *The Regional Geography of the British Caribbean*. At around the 23rd and 24th frames, showing bitumen and bauxite workings, a lively discussion took off to which the whole class was attentive but which was dominated by eight children — Janet, Joyce, Richard, Tina (all white), Clifton, Dorian (both black), and

*It was only later that I came across Lawrence Stenhouse's invaluable elaboration of the idea of the teacher as researcher in chapter 10 of *An Introduction to Curriculum Research and Development* (Heinemann).

Christine and Max (both mixed race). These eight were to play prominent parts in most subsequent discussions.

'Max wanted to know why there were white workers in the bauxite mine. "I thought black men do it," he said. Several black children pointed out there was a mixture of races in the Caribbean. "The Prime Minister is white", one of them said. This was disputed by others who said he was "half-caste" or "light-skinned". Max said something about himself and the Prime Minister which caused ML to ask if he saw himself as white. "No," he answered, "light-skinned". Clifton, returning to Max's original point, suggested that the presence of white workers might be because it was a pre-independence filmstrip ... Dorian said, "Someone told me that white men came and slaved the blacks at Jamaica", and she instanced also television programmes, presumably having the recent slavery series in mind ... Janet spoke up, criticising television for always showing the "bad parts" of Third World countries (not her phrase, but it was obviously what she meant), and she compared the filmstrip favourably with TV in this respect. "Yes," added Richard gesturing, "with their bellies out here". He went on, "if they (ie we in Britain) see the good parts they'll see the West Indies is better ... and all the coloureds would come over here and all the whites would go over there". Someone pointed out that his logic was faulty.

Dorian had been trying to come in for some time. She seemed agitated. When her chance came she said something that didn't sound comprehensible at first. On questioning it appeared she was defending Amin for expelling the Asians from Uganda. "They slaved the blacks", she said. Clifton explained Amin's reasons. Indians, he said, were sending their money out of Uganda to friends in England who could bank it for them. "In that way England was growing richer and Uganda poorer."

The discussion returned to Janet's point about unfair television presentation. What was it really like in the West Indies? Corinne said, "most people were born over here" so they couldn't know what it was like. Dorian disagreed. "It's the reverse. Most black people were born in Jamaica and came over here as children" ...

Joyce had been making what looked like dissenting asides to her neighbour for some time. Finally she came in. "All the coloured children in this school," she said, "are not Jamaican. Their parents are. They have to learn Jamaican. They act big-headed about their parents' country." This observation occasioned so much reaction that the general discussion disappeared from view and small group discussions broke out all over the class. Several members of the class, white as well as black, accused Joyce of being prejudiced. Eventually a single class discussion reasserted itself. Continuing with the language theme Dorian referred to someone who wasn't Jamaican even by parentage talking Jamaican. A white boy (unidentified) said that many children with black fathers and white mothers talked Jamaican. Christine said some people talk Jamaican for a joke.

Joyce insisted that as they were in England they should talk English. "We can speak what we like," said Dorian, "you're jealous". "You're jealous", retorted Richard, "you came over here to our country". Richard spoke at length on immigration. "It's got worse", he concluded, "they should go back". "You cheeky sod", shouted Dorian.

Tina came to the defence of the blacks. "But they were born here. It's their country as much as ours". Clifton reverted to Richard's speech. Whilst admitting he'd made some "shrewd points", he said he was "exaggerating a bit." He explained how at the time of the first immigration from Jamaica conditions had been bad on the island. Now things had improved. Comparing prices in England and Jamaica he said, "England is still better than Jamaica, but only just." This contribution earned Clifton a round of applause.

The question of immigration policy brought up Australia's whites only restriction. Clifton drew the class's attention to the plight of the black aborigines. "They're civilised. People don't understand them so they call them uncivilised" ...

The class returned to the filmstrip. One of the final frames was of white West Indians. Earlier Joyce had argued that, since white people didn't go to the Caribbean to live, black people shouldn't come here. When the frame came up, a couple of black girls rounded on Joyce. "We've got you back, Joyce", one said triumphantly, "that shows you".

At the end of the lesson Tina said to ML she didn't think "we should be doing this work. It might cause offence to the coloured children in the class". ML asked the "coloured" children if they

agreed. None of them did. Clifton commented that it was only
Joyce who was likely to cause difficulty, and Tina accused her of
being "colour-prejudiced". Joyce denied it indignantly.'

Early observation of the class naturally produced some first impres-
sions. One of the most striking was of interracial harmony. The
headteacher, ML and all the other teachers in the school I spoke to
voiced the opinion that, taking the outside world into account,
relations between black and white in the school were comparatively
good. They certainly appeared to be so in the class on first
acquaintance. Where the children sat and the way they behaved
towards one another both suggested a norm of natural interracial
mixing. Equally striking was the good relationship existing between
the class and ML; integral to this was the kind of open discussion he
had established as an enjoyable and valuable method of teaching
and learning.

There were a number of features of this first discussion, both in
the way it was handled by the teacher and in the way it was handled
by the class, which were to prove typical. Two aspects of ML's
method were distinctive. First, he allowed the children very largely
to dictate the course of the debate. Nothing any child said was
rejected or diverted on the grounds of irrelevance; such control as
he exerted resided in the kind of questions he asked. Surprisingly
perhaps this did not lead to discussion becoming wayward or
haphazard. What it did result in was freedom for the children to
compare the content of the curriculum with their own knowledge
and experience. For example, in a later lesson looking at conditions
on the slave ships Clifton, a black boy and the class's political
expert, drew parallels with contemporary events. 'It's like in Russia
now,' he said. 'If you make a joke about someone in the Kremlin,
they put you in prison.'; and he went on to cite the case of the
scientist Sakharov not being given a visa to collect his Nobel prize.
Consider also the way talking about race arose naturally out of the
filmstrip. That part of the discussion was in no sense engineered by
ML; he merely allowed it to develop. Equally natural was the way
talking about the Caribbean moved into talking about blacks in
Britain and, in later discussions, the way talking about slavery
moved into talking about prejudice and discrimination today.

The second distinctive aspects of ML's method was the belief,
implicit in his handling of this and all other observed lessons, that
on no account must race, or any facet of race (even the most
delicate), become taboo. Tina at the end of the lesson expressed the

anxieties of many teachers when she queried whether the Caribbean unit might not be offensive to the "coloured" children, but she was alone in the class in her opinion and it was one she was later to disown. Indeed, the evidence of the lesson itself suggested that the class was well able to accommodate even confrontational debate within its tacit philosophy of interracial harmony. The tenor of the discussion was notably amicable. At times it certainly became heated and hard things were said, but all was given and taken in good part. Dorian's retort to Richard, 'You cheeky sod', was the only personal insult recorded during the observation period, and there was never anything approaching the bouts of racial slanging other teachers have reported from their classrooms. If there was a cause for concern it was the class's treatment of Joyce. Admittedly she made negative statements on immigration and on the use of Creole, but then so did Tina and Richard (albeit in their case combined with and outweighed by more positive ones) and the labelling of her as prejudiced seemed both unjust and oversimple. Unfortunately this description was to harden into a firm stereotype, and it would not be too fanciful to say that by the end of the term Joyce had become something of a scapegoat for the class's anxieties about race.

In addition to Joyce several other children who flourished in discussion emerged as characters with distinctive roles to play. Clifton contributed more to discussions than any other individual, both in quantity and quality. He was noticeably more knowledgeable and aware than anyone else, an achievement he managed to combine with reasonableness and charm, although even he was guilty in the general injustice done to Joyce. Dorian was more volatile and militant. In debate, but not on paper, she was the strongest black champion of black rights. The white champion was Janet, who, though not entirely consistent in her position, was markedly more so than Tina or Richard. These two, whilst on the whole conforming to the class norm, oscillated between tolerance and intolerance in their spoken and written utterances. Max was often to attract attention, not just because he was a source of what disturbances there were, but also because it was frequently he who raised, as he did on this first occasion, the issue of race. It has also to be said that, although the whole class was invariably attentive to what was going on, a significant minority contributed little or nothing to the animated discussions that took place.

2 The second extract is from a lesson in which ML read the class

five passages from Paula Fox's novel about the transatlantic slave trade, *The Slave Dancer*. The first passage described the kidnapping of the white hero, Jessie, in New Orleans; the second his sensations at sea for the first time; the third the boarding of the slaves in the Bight of Benin; the fourth Jessie's first playing of the pipe for the slaves to dance to; and the fifth the brutal punishment of a rebellious slave.

'In the first passage one of the white sailors used the word "nigger" pejoratively. No class reaction... Tina interrupted the third passage to ask what colour Jessie was. She hadn't realised he was white... After the fourth passage and in connexion with the maltreatment of the black slaves Richard said, "In films black slaves seem to be enjoying working for white masters... They're always smiling". "They'll have to", said Clifton, "or they'll get lashed... That's all they've been given to enjoy, might as well make the best of what they'd got." Janet asked if they weren't actually "better off" as slaves in the West Indies than at home in Africa. ML said life on the plantations was as bad as life on the slave ships.

Later on Janet commented: "The whites hardly dare touch the blacks nowadays. Some of the coloured might want revenge for slavery". Clifton agreed, but said some blacks and whites got on well. Hence intermarriage, suggested Janet... Tina and Clifton reckoned that race relations were bad in Liverpool (as distinct from this city) and in the United States. "In some parts of the USA," said Janet, "they really respect the coloured but not in Philadelphia where my cousin lives. Whites spit on coloureds there". Max found this hard to believe.

ML asked for a definition of prejudice. Janet thought it meant being against "coloureds". Others said it could be any group. Clifton cited the treatment of the Chinese, ML of the Jews. Tina said she'd heard a lot of people say Jews were "spiteful people" and she referred to the colloquial expression "tight as a Jew". Janet pointed out that Jesus was a Jew.

Richard recounted his aunt's experience of segregation on buses in the USA. Robert said his cousin couldn't go to South Africa because he'd married an Indian girl.

At the end of the lesson Gabrielle borrowed *The Slave Dancer* to read for herself.'

Spontaneously discussion of the maltreatment of slaves was transformed into discussion of the contemporary racial situation in Britain and elsewhere. To Janet must go the credit for introducing the idea that hostility between blacks and whites today is in some sense a legacy of slavery. It was a theme that was to recur throughout the assessment period.

Another recurring theme which appeared for the first time in this lesson was that race relations were better in this city than others and better in Britain than in countries such as the United States and South Africa. At the end of the lesson ML asked the class to write a story about the slave trade for homework. The four best were written by black and mixed race children — Christine (G), Gary, Maria and Max. Gary's and Maria's are reproduced here in their entirety.

Gary's story

'I was with my mother in our hut when the chief of the tribe sent for us. When we reached the chief's hut it had white men inside. We had heard of these white men but we had never seen one before. Outside the hut we saw the rest of our family in chains. We were shocked. All of a sudden we were grabbed and put into chains as well by other white men.

"What is this?" I squealed. I looked around and a whip came swishing across my face. I bawled out loud and a white man came up to me and kicked my shin. My mother told me to be quiet and stay near her.

After about a mile's walk we came to a beach. There were lots of little boats and we were all bundled on, twenty to a boat. Fortunately I was loaded on the same boat as the rest of my family. Then we were put on to a big ship. There were screams everywhere but we were soon quietened down by the tails of the whip.

On the ship we had hardly any food to eat. We had to dance to a tune played by a flute. Some people threw fits and went charging at the white men, but when they stopped their hysterics they were whipped till the skin on their backs was almost torn apart. If people moaned and groaned in the night when the white men were sleeping they would get flogged too. Most of the people wished they were dead and tried to kill themselves regularly.

This was the time when slave selling was illegal and there was always a man on the lookout for ships that were on the lookout for them. But one day there was a ship sighted by one of the white men. The slaves were getting thrown overboard so that the white men would not get caught. There were screams everywhere. All of my family (including me) were grabbed by a group of white men to be thrown overboard. My father and mother struggled in vain. We were the last ones left. Black bodies were floating in the water. I was screaming and kicked a white man in his shins although my legs were chained. My father punched and scratched the white men in their faces and they whipped him until finally we gave up. We were thrown overboard. The more we struggled the more we sank. We could not breathe. Down we went. My little sister had died already. I was the next youngest so that meant I was the next to go. Then everything went blank.'

Maria's story

'I woke up opening my eyes slowly. I rubbed them, then I stood up and stretched stiffly. One of the native guards outside brought in a dish of cold rice and a bowl of water. I drank some of the water then I started to eat the rice. As I ate I thought about what had happened the past four days. The battle, the burning of the huts, the slaughter of men, women and children. About 70 or 80 people had been spared and taken back to the conquering tribe's village, to be sold as slaves. I ate another mouthful of rice then I looked about me. Some of the people on the floor were stirring. They stood up and started eating and drinking as well. The men were in this hut and the women in another. There was some straw on the floor on which we slept. The only fresh air came through the cracks in the door. I finished eating then stretched again. I heard the sound of men approaching, then the clinking of chains. I knew that we were to be sold now. The door of the hut opened. About 10 white men entered. They were all carrying whips. They made everyone stand up then they shackled us all together, barking out orders in a language we couldn't understand. Then with a fair amount of whipping they got everyone moving. We walked for about 2 miles. The sun was high now over the hills. The men saw we were getting tired so they stopped for a rest. We were all given water. After about twenty minutes we started moving again. At last we reached the ship. The sides were high and it was difficult to hold on. With lots of whipping the men managed to get us all on board. The women we lifted on.

We were then thrown down inside the ship. The place we were thrown in smelt of damp and mustiness. There was also a smell of unwashed bodies. There wasn't much space to move about in as the hold was all of 7 feet long and about 3 feet wide. The floor was just bare wooden boards. The men then chained us all together. They brought down food (if you can call it that). It was rice (several days old judging by the taste) with oil and pepper. Not many of us would have eaten it but we'd had no food since that morning. Then they shut up the hold. It was dark and the circulation of fresh air stopped.

Day by day some of the women and the weaker men died. The only exercise we got was being taken on deck and made to dance. Conditions slowly got worse. The food we got was often in a rotten condition.

One day the captain gave orders to his crew to start feeding the slaves better. "Get more for them if they're in good condition". So instead of the usual cold rice and oil we had rice and salt beef. We had, I imagine, been travelling for about two months when at last we reached our destination. The hold was opened up into the daylight. At first we closed our eyes not used to the strong light of the sun. But gradually our eyes got used to it. We were then put on the quay.

As I looked around I saw a lot of white children who were looking at us, spitting and throwing rubbish, but the captain soon put a stop to that. We were taken into a large building which had large wooden tubs in it. We were all made to undress and have a wash in the tubs. The water was icy cold. After we were given clean clothes and food. We were taken into another part of the building and were shown places to sleep.

The next morning we were woken early and taken to another building. We were made to stand on this wooden stage. The hall gradually filled with people. Then the bidding got under way. As each one was sold they were branded with the owner's initials. I was sold to one owner of a plantation which grew sugar cane and cotton. The man was about 40 to 45 years old. He had small eyes hidden in the folds of his fleshy face. He had a few warts on his nose. He looked cruel. I was branded and shackled. Then taken to the plantation to start a new life.'

It is perhaps no surprise, given the link provided by racial ancestry, that the most graphic and felt stories should have been written by black and mixed race children. What may well surprise, and indeed prompt criticism, is the overwhelmingly bleak and pessimistic picture conveyed. The resistance of the slaves in Gary's story is frantic and futile and their ultimate death seems inevitable, but somehow preferable, if only as a release, to the 'new life' on the plantation ironically announced at the conclusion to Maria's. In striking these emphases on suffering and degradation the children were, of course, simply taking their cue from the unit's material on the transatlantic middle passage and from the excerpts read to them from *The Slave Dancer*; and it is on this ground, the unbalanced selection of historical content, that the unit primarily left itself open to criticism.

3 A week later the class were looking at a passage describing life on the sugar plantations. An interesting discussion began at the point where it mentioned that white overseers and book-keepers, discouraged from marriage, took slave mistresses and produced 'mulatto' children.

'ML asked the class what today's term for such children was. They were unanimous that it was "half-caste". They also said "quarter-caste" was used, but it was not clear whether it applied to a child with three black grandparents and one white as well as to a child with three white grandparents and one black. There was some disagreement as to whether "half-caste" was also used for other racial mixtures, for example black and Chinese. Clifton said his father used "light-skinned" instead of "half-caste", and ML wondered whether there wasn't a suggestion of insult about the phrase. None of the children thought so.

ML asked the class for their views on interracial marriage. Janet said, "Only prejudiced people think it's wrong", and she pointed to Joyce who protested. Richard expressed the general class view when he said, "If you've got feelings for someone and you love them, why shouldn't you?"

Paul referred to a "light-coloured" boy being called names by "coloured" people. Max said he'd heard someone say to a "half-caste" boy that his mum must have been "hard-up" to marry a black man. Tina had seen a fight outside the library between a black woman and a white woman. The black woman had attacked and beaten up the white woman for having an affair with her husband. She'd shouted, "If you want a black man, go and get your own". Christine (G) told a story about a white girl and her black boyfriend and her mother not approving.

ML asked who in the class would describe themselves as "half-caste". Christine, Corinne and Max all put their hands up. Maria the other mixed race child, was away. ML asked them what they felt about it. Max said, "When I was born, I was a bit darker than Christine. I thought I was coloured. But when I grew up I came out like this". (Max is very fair-skinned.) ML commented on the difference between Christine's wiry African hair and Corinne's straighter European hair.

Janet reckoned that "half-castes" sometimes have a lot of friends of both races. Tina thought people generally lump them with "coloureds", and that they form a single group.

Sharon told a story of a group of coloured girls making fun of a mixed race family... Clifton said he knew a Jamaican woman who'd got lighter in England ...

Christine suddenly announced, "My gran is Irish", and Max said, "My dad's got marks on his back". He added that his dad was African and thought the marks might have something to do with slavery! ... ML said to all the black and mixed race children, "All of your ancestors came from Africa originally". No-one demurred, except Dorian, but she'd misunderstood him to mean her parents.'

Sex, intermarriage and mixed race children are emotive facets of the race question, and an area pervaded by myths and stereotypes. The lesson is a good illustration of ML's refusal to allow such an area to be dominated by taboo, even at the risk of touching sensitive nerves in the mixed race children themselves. In the very first lesson he had asked Max whether he thought of himself as white, and in this third lesson excerpt he was able to create a climate in which Max, Christine and Corinne (Maria was absent) felt confident enough to talk about the experience of being between two races.

4 Since the content of the Caribbean unit had so consistently raised issues to do with racial prejudice, ML and the class decided that a lesson towards the end of term should be given over entirely to a discussion of the whole vexed question. The final notebook extract covers part of that discussion.

'Clifton started the ball rolling by saying that the origins of prejudice lay in "jealousy". Richard supported him. "The coloureds are sort of jealous of us because they came over here". Dorian retorted, "The whites came to Jamaica so they must have been jealous of us"

ML asked why West Indians had come to Britain. Richard answered, "To start a new life". Gabrielle said it was because there were "poor facilities in Africa". Corrected over "Africa", she said that the West Indies must have had "economic difficulties".

ML asked why "people haven't come from everywhere". Corinne pointed out that the West Indies had been "part of England", and Clifton added that there had been assisted passages for West Indians because "they wanted West Indians over here, to help us get richer" ...

Clifton expressed disapproval of colonialism — "pinching other people's islands" — and asked if the British Empire had been bigger than the Roman. Richard argued that the British had succeeded as imperialists because "they had better equipment and heavy armour; the Indians only had a cloth covering their private parts".

Several children stated that colonialism was wrong — Clifton, "They should have left them to themselves"; Janet, "Each country should be left to its own nationality"; Robert, "The Arawaks were there first". Corinne dissented slightly, "But, sir, if they had a disease, British doctors helped them". ML took up the point of whether colonialism hadn't done some good. Someone (unidentified) said it would be good for a poor country like Bangladesh. ML asked if the rights and wrongs had anything to do with the *way* colonizing was done.

Andrew said, "You should make a deal with the chief — negotiate". Richard agreed, "Yes, trade and tell him we'll help him rule the island and protect him from the Spaniards." "They should have laid down their arms", said Janet, "to show they came in peace". ML asked why it hadn't happened like this. "The sailors saw people dancing round totem poles", Richard said, "and must have thought they were uncivilised" ...

ML asked, "What do you think it was like for black people seeing whites for the first time?" Janet answered, "They'd think they were like bad tribes"; and Richard, "They'd think the same as whites of blacks".

Anthony told a story of how a white boy had commented on his skin colour when he was in primary school — "must have been in the sun a long time" — and expressed surprise that his blood was red when he cut himself. "I thumped him", said Anthony dispassionately. "You're surprised at black people," Janet remembered, "when you're little".

ML wanted to know why Anthony had got so "mad" with the white boy. "He was getting cheeky", was the reply. Dorian said she also hit people who called her names, and it was agreed in the class that this was right. "Have any of you coloured kids thought about whites being odd?" ML asked. No answer.

Gabrielle compared crude ideas of other races to her own childish idea when younger, that the heart was actually shaped as in Valentine cards. ML asked about racial myths in comics and films. "White people are presented as kings", said Clifton, "Like in cowboys and Indians. White men killed off the buffaloes, so Indians had a right to fight back."

ML referred to Tarzan films, "You never see the white men carrying the baggage". "That shows them using us", said Dorian, "And taking the mickey out of us. Now people like Amin are getting their own back."

"Isn't Amin prejudiced?" asked ML. "Not really", said Clifton, "He had his reasons," and he repeated his explanation, given in an earlier lesson, of the expulsion of the Ugandan Asians, and he added, "When he was going to kill that journalist, he made the Queen send James Callaghan."

Anthony told another of his stories, this time about a teacher in his primary school who'd called him and other black boys "niggers". Joyce said she'd heard a teacher in her school call some children "black pigs". "Some teachers don't like black children", commented Clifton.

Richard had been thinking about Anthony's story. "I'd be naughty all the time if I'd been in Anthony's position". Admitting he occasionally addressed black boys in his fourth year tutor group as "Sambo" for a joke, ML said, "I wouldn't *treat* black kids any different from whites". "Some teachers do though",

Clifton repeated and he commented that using "Sambo" as a jokey form of address was "all right as long as you don't go too far."

Paul made one of his rare statements. "A lot of people think my sister is prejudiced because she speaks her mind."'

This discussion differed from its predecessors in the obvious sense that it was the result of a conscious decision taken by ML and the class; the necessity for it had arisen out of the insight, first publicly achieved by Janet, that one of the legacies of the slave trade was racism. What was interesting was the way a discussion of racial prejudice today moved back in time to a discussion of the rights and wrongs of colonialism, whereas in previous discussions the movement had been in the opposite direction — from the past to the present. When the class returned to the present, they returned to schools and to the first open inroad into the notion of their school as a racially harmonious institution, for it was quite evident that in talking about prejudice among teachers the children, black and white, were not excluding the ones teaching them at the time. In none of the observed lessons did ML confine his role to that of a detached chairman, but he was much more of a participant in this duscussion than others and, in addition, a participant *on equal terms* with the children. It was not just that he allowed them to air their views on staff attitudes in general, but that in candidly admitting to weaknesses in his own practice (calling black teenagers 'Sambo' as a joke) he invited, and accepted, the reproof implicit in Clifton's, 'That's all right as long as you don't go too far.'

Towards the end of the lesson ML asked the class to jot down their thoughts and feelings about racial prejudice. Several of the children found this difficult. Anthony and Max said they were still unsure what prejudice was. Gary paused from his writing to ask ML if Enoch Powell was prejudiced. ML said it was not an easy question; he would say 'Yes' but others would disagree. A bit later Richard leaned across to Max and asked, 'Max, do you like light-skinned people'? 'Course I do,' said Max.

The written work, when analysed, covered the reasons for prejudice, the rights and wrongs of it, what can be done about it, and how the writers saw it in relation to themselves. The general class view was that the origins of prejudice lay in jealousy and ignorance and that prejudiced people were daft, mad or foolish. If there was uncertainty about the exact meaning of prejudice, there was virtual unanimity that it was wrong and we are all human beings. Only Paul admitted to being prejudiced, and he failed to elaborate. A few others said they used to be but had changed recently, in some cases as a result of the Caribbean work. Christine (G) wrote that she was 'a little prejudiced once against people like Chinese or Pakistanis', and Dorian confessed that she didn't like the way Indians and Pakistanis 'go and smell' but she liked them in other unspecified ways. The strongest expression of the general class view was from Janet:

> 'I think it was wrong to go and make fun of the blacks because they are just as civilised as us. I have learnt a lot from all this prejudice stuff and I think to go all them places and kill and collect the black people was one of the most cruel things ever done. I think that people who are prejudiced are just trying to identify their own colour ... Why should there be prejudice when everyone is the same as everyone else? The only thing that is different is the colour. And there is no better brains involved neither because some black people are brainier than white and some white people are brainier than black people.'

Christine (G), identifying herself interestingly, was more perceptive than most about the nature of prejudice, 'We thought ourselves to be better, in a sort of higher position, and thought only of them as people who are only fit to be slaves.' Roger was the only black child to make a distinctively black contribution: 'If white people call me bad names I just call them back names. Sometimes I hit them ... Sometimes when black people think of good names for themselves like Black Power some whites don't like that.'

Questionnaires and interviews

At the end of the unit the whole class completed questionnaires, and ten children were interviewed on tape for about fifteen minutes each. The intention was to ascertain what they had learned from the Caribbean unit and whether they had appreciated it or not. Prior knowledge was shown to have been pretty negligible. The white children's had been limited to the fact that black people came to Britain and, in a few cases, that slaves had been taken from Africa to work on plantations in the Caribbean. The black and mixed race children claimed, on the whole, no more. Trevor, for instance, said in his interview that the Unit's content had all been news to him because, even though he asked his parents about the

West Indies from time to time, they had been away from the islands for fifteen years. Dorian, on the other hand, had been told something about slavery by her parents and also about their own lives in Jamaica:

> 'When they used to go to school they had to walk miles and miles barefoot, with no shoes, and before they had to go to school they had to go over the hill to fetch some water and come back again or else they'd get hit with a cane.'

The real exception was Wendy, understandably enough, who said there was nothing in the unit she had not previously been taught in her Barbados school.

Although the class as a whole learned a good deal from the unit, the questionnaires and the interviews revealed gaps, confusions and uncertainties in their knowledge. On the slave trade, for example, condemnation was widespread. Richard summed it up when he wrote, 'the slave trade was a brutal attack on peaceful negroes.' But vagueness and muddle pervaded some accounts of who enslaved whom and whence and whither the slaves were taken. Only one child actually said 'the slave people were African.' One wrote that they were 'mostly black', and another wondered if a few had not been white. Two children were specific about the provenance of the slavers — one that they were white, the other that they were British. Several children wrote that the slavers took the slaves from South Africa, (another said South America); two that they were taken to be slaves in England; and Andrew that they had been taken *from* and not *to* Jamaica. On the manner of their transportation the minority who discussed it felt they had been 'more or less took', but one child suggested they might have gone voluntarily. There was little reference to the triangular nature of the Atlantic trade, and only one lucid version of its underlying economics.

The class' opinion of the unit was very favourable almost without exceptions. 'Good,' 'interesting', 'educational', 'learnt a lot', 'helped me a lot', 'exciting', 'very worthwhile', were typical comments. One child praised the variety of the work — 'something different every lesson', and especially popular were the modelling of an Arawaks' village and the discussions. In the opinion of Jacqueline and Joyce the discussions had enabled the 'whole truth' to emerge. 'You do not get the chance to say the truth anywhere else,' said Joyce. A good aspect of the discussion, Jacqueline thought, was that 'when we have an argument in class it is a friendly argument not a quarrel.' Clifton, on the other hand, felt that some people in the more 'heated' arguments had got 'a bit out of hand'. But, he admitted, 'I found out some things about myself.'

Dislikes were mainly restricted to the content of study. Anthony, for example, wrote,

> 'I didn't like the part about the slavery and how they got split from their family, how they got beatings if they did not do their work, how they spied on each other when one of them tried to escape.'

Gary, too, had not liked the 'nastiness' of the slave trade, nor the slaughtering of the Arawaks by the Spaniards. Other children had been 'shocked' or 'surprised' by what they had learned. Janet said she was surprised 'the blacks have not got their own back on us yet after what we did to them.' The maturest criticism came from Robert. He wrote that there had been too much on history, especially on certain aspects like slavery, and not enough on 'today's Caribbean' and 'the time when the slaves were set free.'

A dislike of a different kind was expressed by Joyce. She referred slightingly to those in the class who had said "white people are prejudiced."

RJ: 'What did you think about that?'

J: 'It's not right.'

RJ: 'One or two said you are, didn't they? Right at the beginning. (Joyce nods) Why do you think they said that?'

J: 'I don't know ... I'm not because I wouldn't go around with them (if I was).'

RJ: 'Do you have a lot of black friends?'

J: 'That's the most I've got.'

The way Joyce became stereotyped as the prejudiced member of the class has already been commented on. The statements she made after the first discussion which were quite clearly not prejudiced appeared to be disregarded by her classmates because they did not tally with the picture of her they had already decided on. Dorian and Christine, in their interview, both referred spontaneously to the first discussion. Dorian remembered how the filmstrip had disproved Joyce's idea that all West Indians are black — 'so we caught her out on that and I was laughing.' Christine was less malicious — 'when the filmstrip came on she was surprised, I think.'

Joyce was not the only child to jolt the norm of interracial harmony. Andrew also struck a discordant note. Asked for his views on Jamaicans speaking Creole, he said he did not mind so long as they did not criticize him:

'They call me a white honky and things like that ... Sometimes the
coloureds just run about, kick you off ... Wahid (a Pakistani
friend) was in the playground and he had his bag round his neck
and a coloured boy came up and pulled him over by his bag.'

Conclusions

By the end of the assessment period I did not feel disposed to draw
any firm conclusions, since it had proved increasingly difficult to be
sure that the data thrown up was anything more than superficial.
Two factors in particular appeared to be obstructions in the way of
getting to the heart of what the Caribbean unit was doing for the
children.

In the first place just under half of the class contributed little or
nothing to the discussions, so it was impossible to know what their
attitudes were, for instance, to the norms of interracial harmony
and equal rights quickly established by their talkative classmates.
Perhaps their silence signified consent, but two quiet white children
(Paul in his writing and Andrew in his interview) struck discordant
notes. Moreover, among the talkative white children, three —
Joyce, Richard and Tina — were inconsistent in their pronouncements, oscillating between tolerance and intolerance, which casts
some doubt on the assumption underlying attitude assessment that
children of this age (and indeed adults) all have coherent attitudes
which can be inferred from what they say and write.

Secondly, it was especially difficult to be certain about the
reactions of the quieter black and mixed race children (that is to
say, all except for Christine, Clifton, Dorian and Max). Whereas
some of the white children seemed to be holding back because they
did not wish to be seen at odds with the established group norms,
the taciturnity of the minority race children seemed to be due to a
reluctance to expose their racial identities to classroom investigation. Either they felt unsure or ambivalent towards their identities,
or else they needed to be convinced first that they were valued by
the school and the class. Even in the one to one interviews there was a
feeling that one or two children were not prepared to risk sensitive
aspects of their identities — their language, say, or their ancestry —
with a white interlocutor. The same sort of motivation was perhaps
responsible for the spoken and written remarks made by some black
children which asked to be taken other than at face value or which
seemed designed to fit in with what their authors took to be the
expectations of others.

Nevertheless the force of the assessment evidence did seem strong enough to substantiate serious reservations I had about the unit's selection of objectives and content. In the first place I questioned whether wholly cognitive objectives, limited to knowledge and understanding (which is what the unit's were), could be adequate for a unit on the Caribbean in a school with a significant minority of children of West Indian ancestry. Affective objectives were surely necessary too — covering, broadly speaking, the identity and self-respect of black and mixed race children and the respect of other children for the historical and cultural achievements of the Caribbean.* Secondly, the application of affective objectives of this kind as touchstones pointed to omissions and deficiencies in the unit's selection of historical content.

The only member of the class to express explicit criticism of the content was a white boy, Robert, but the written and spoken comments of others — notably Anthony, Dorian and Gary (all of whom were black) — bore implicit reproach. Robert criticised the historical imbalance (too much on slavery and not enough on emancipation and after) and the absence of material on 'today's Caribbean', while the three black children had been deeply affected by the wholly negative presentation of the black experience of slavery which had led Dorian, for example, to believe that black people had not fought against it. It is vital that both black and white children should know that blacks did more about slavery than suffer it supinely. They need to know about escapes, mutinies, rebellions and the black role in the emancipation struggle. Full and interesting coverage of the highlights of black resistance — of Toussaint L'Ouverture, the Maroons, and the Morant Bay rebellion, to name but three — are provided in parts one, two and five of Book 3 of *The People Who Came*, (Longman) and three historical novels intended for younger secondary school pupils and dealing respectively with the same highlights — Morna Stuart's *Marassa and Midnight* (Heinemann) and Vic Reid's *The Young Warriors* and *Sixty-Five* (Longman) — could serve as useful supplementary material. The absence of this kind of material explains the failure of the whole class in their questionnaires to name any famous black people apart from sportsmen and entertainers.

Another important omission in the content was a positive treatment of the African connexion. Many teachers believe that

---

*This was my view at the time. It is not my view now, three years later, as will be apparent from the discussion in other chapters.

Caribbean children cannot boast of a distinctive cultural heritage, in the sense that Asian children can, because what their ancestors took from Africa was effectively destroyed by slavery. Whilst it is undoubtedly true that black children tend on the whole to be less sure of their cultural identities, and that slavery severely disrupted the original African cultures of the slaves, the work of West Indian historians has shown that an African-based folk culture flourished among the slaves and still survives in the Caribbean today despite the attrition wreaked by the European-orientated education of the colonial period after emancipation.[2] Since this study was undertaken, the idea of the unbroken continuity of the black experience has, of course, become both more available and more acceptable following the publicity captured by Rastafarianism, reggae and the television version of Alex Haley's *Roots*.

The final major criticism referred to the level of understanding attained by the children. Three important elements in the way the unit was realised were slavery, immigration and racial prejudice. Although one of the class's main achievements was their insight into the relationship between these three phenomena, it seemed doubtful whether their understanding ever became complete enough. For instance, they grasped only half the story of West Indian immigration into Britain. Whilst they knew that it had been partly prompted by economic problems in the Caribbean, there was very little understanding of the 'pull' factors operating from Britain or of the function of immigrant workers in the British labour market. The understanding of racism was equally limited, and it is possible that the complex ramifications to such a concept are beyond most children of this age. Nevertheless the class had understood that slavery and colonialism were historical determinants, and on different occasions Gabrielle and Janet identified the belief in the inferiority of black people as the kernel of the concept. So it is particularly unfortunate that so many of the class should have been able to escape with the superficial view that racial prejudice is some kind of mental aberration — the monopoly of the jealous, the daft and the mad.

The justice of these criticisms was conceded by the teachers responsible for the unit, and considerable changes were made to its content for the following year in order to meet them. I do not wish now to detract from the force of these criticisms, nor to qualify seriously the claim already put (in the previous chapter) that the essential educational decisions concern the content of the curriculum. But I should like to revert to my initial point about the centrality of the curriculum's social context to its success. I have tried to show that the overall harmony of classroom relationships enabled the teacher to extract maximum benefit from the open style of discussion to which he attached such importance. The discussions were 'open' in two senses. First, children who wanted to say something were allowed relatively free rein which meant that to a large extent they dictated the direction of debate. Not that the teacher forsook his conventional role of arbiter and chairman entirely. Discussion was sometimes initiated at his discretion, and the questions he asked exerted some control on the way in which it went. Where he did forsake his role, it was to be a participant. On these occasions he was clearly seen by the class as an individual with opinions and attitudes. This they welcomed; they wanted to know where he stood. But there was never any suggestion, on his part or theirs, that his views carried greater weight than theirs by dint of his status as a teacher.

The other striking feature of the discussions (the other sense in which they were 'open') lay in the teacher's determination not to allow any semblance of taboo to accrue to any facet of the issue of race. This resulted, for instance, in the classroom exploration of the situation of mixed race children, something many teachers would be anxious to avoid for fear of hurting the sensibilities of the children themselves. Many teachers would also be anxious to avoid black/white confrontation over race in the classroom on similar grounds. Tina voiced this anxiety in the first observed lesson when she said that the Caribbean work might 'cause offence to the coloured children.' As it turned out the only child who gave any obvious sign of being hurt or offended was a white one, Joyce. By the time the assessment period ended the injustice done to Joyce by the class had not been publicly acknowledged or expiated.

Although the discussions were frequently heated, black/white confrontation was, given the nature of the subject matter, surprisingly rare, and complete racial polarisation never occurred. There were always one or two of the talkative children on the 'wrong' side of the divide, and, most significantly, the kind of racial slurs which, on Andrew's evidence, were traded in the playground were not traded in the classroom. No doubt in other classrooms, with different racial compositions and less harmonious relationships, discussion of the type encouraged by this teacher might well have had counterproductive and damaging effects. But, in this one classroom, it seemed, by and large, to work for the teacher and for the children who, as the questionnaires and interviews show valued it for its combination of truthfulness and goodnaturedness.

I do not wish to make exaggerated claims for the discussions. In one way, for example, they were too traditional. The fact that they were always conducted in the forum of the whole class necessarily meant that only a proportion of the class could ever be active participants. Nevertheless their 'openness' did seem to me authentic; and it does represent a major pedagogic achievement.

I have argued in earlier parts of the book for the need for teachers to be 'open' to their pupils' cultural experience and to what they know and think about race. I want now to start to argue for the development of classrooms which are 'open' in further senses. First, teachers need to establish, as the teacher in the study clearly had, classroom climates which strike pupils as sufficiently 'open' for them to say and write what they genuinely feel; and secondly, teachers need themselves to be 'open' to what actually happens in the classroom when the curriculum they have planned is realised. For, only if they are, can they even begin to evaluate its effects.

References

1   It is impossible to overstate my indebtedness to Martin Locke, the teacher involved in this study.
2   See, for example, Edward Brathwaite *Folk Culture of the Slaves in Jamaica* (New Beacon) and Leonard Barrett *The Sun and the Drum* (Heinemann).

4 From Theory to Practice

'a curriculum made only of teachers' intentions would be an insubstantial thing from which nobody would learn much. To become meaningful a curriculum has to be enacted by pupils as well as teachers....'
Douglas Barnes

The theory of the chapter's title is the theory elaborated and discussed in chapter 2 and the practice that of teaching English in a small downtown secondary school in the West Midlands. The previous two chapters have initiated an exploration of the relationship between theory and practice, in the shape of setting curriculum models against classroom realities and adjudging the relative importance of content and process. I want now to try and crystallise this by presenting and evaluating two years of my own teaching experience.

Given sufficient knowledge, money and power, some of the things that need to be done towards multiracialising an English curriculum are comparatively easily accomplished. As head of an English department for the past two years, indeed as the school's only qualified teacher of English, I have had the authority and at least some of the money I wanted to start changing the virtually all-white content of the stock cupboard and the school library; whilst my three years on the Schools Council Multiracial Education project provided me with the necessary knowledge and criteria for book selection (already listed in chapter 2). Easily achieved also, although obviously it takes time and some thoughtful experimentation, is what might be called a 'paper' curriculum — the kind of thing headteachers and visiting inspectors will expect to be given a copy of — that is, a statement of objectives and a syllabus specifying year by year the topics and themes which the multiracial materials are to service.

I have recorded in chapter 2 that it was eighteen months before I felt disposed to attempt a delineation of objectives, so it was something which came at the end rather than at the beginning of my particular piece of curriculum development, but it seems logical to start a description there. In its final form the list read as follows:

Aims and objectives for the teaching of English

Overall Aim

Pupils should achieve competence in the understanding, appreciation and use of English for personal fulfilment, social survival and action, and rewarding relationships with others.

Cognitive Objectives: (a) Skills

Pupils should be able to:

Listening	listen attentively, sensitively and with discrimination.
Talking	communicate successfully in a variety of contexts.
Reading	realise their full potential for reading with understanding;
	identify the salient points in a piece of writing;
	use reference books and other sources of information;
	read aloud clearly, fluently and expressively;
	evaluate critically the various contemporary uses of English;
	respond sensitively to the implications of meaning, form and style.
Writing	write legibly;
	spell correctly;
	structure effectively sentences, paragraphs and more sustained pieces of writing;
	synthesize in their own words points extracted from a passage or from reference material;
	write in a variety of registers appropriate to different contexts;
	master the basic forms of literary expression — story, play, poem.

Cognitive Objectives: (b) Knowledge

Pupils should know:

> the history of the English language;
> that English has many dialects (including Standard English) and accents (including Received Pronounciation), none of which is linguistically superior to any other.

Affective Objectives

Pupils should:
(if English is their mother tongue) take pride in their own form of it;
take pleasure in reading;
derive enjoyment from and take pride in their own writing;
respond positively to the form and content of literature;
appreciate the richness of the English language;
through literature share empathetically in the experiences and viewpoints of others.

This list is open to the usual criticism levelled at lists of objectives of being banal and unexceptionable (although, somewhat to my surprise, one or two items have proved in practice highly controversial), but what was rewarding for me was not so much the end product as the process by which it was reached. My list is in fact based on an original drawn up by seven heads of English, including myself, after three days of intensive discussion on a DES course to do with the assessment of English in secondary schools. Most of the group taught in urban areas, with at least a small percentage of minority race pupils, but one was head of English in a rural grammar school. It was no small achievement for us eventually to have settled on a common set of goals — equally applicable to inner city multiracial schools and rural all-white ones. It will come as no surprise, in the light of the discussion in chapter 2, that I fully endorsed the weighting in favour of skills objectives, and at no point argued for specifically multiracial attitudinal objectives such as promoting interracial respect. I think it would be fair to claim, however, that the second knowledge objective and the first and last affective objectives bear the imprint of my multiracial preoccupations.

The finalization of a syllabus, in the sense of a complete statement of the themes and topics to be covered over five years and the books and materials to be used to service them, is obviously an even longer process. All I can offer are the kinds of ideas I have experimented with and found successful.

By and large I have opted for traditional, not to say time-honoured, themes representing salient aspects of human experience which both lend themselves to multiracialisation and at the same time do not run the risk of striking white children as partisan — not 'for them'. It is absolutely crucial that the themes which constitute a curriculum's organising principle should speak equally to all children — alienating no one and offering each something to relate to or compare with his or her own experience.

Examples of English topics suitable for the multiracial classroom

Topic	Lead novel(s)	Year
Home and school	Michael Baldwin *Grandad with Snails*	First
	Bernard Ashley *The Trouble with Donovan Croft*	
Adventure	VS Reid *The Young Warriors*	First
	Peter Dickinson *The Devil's Children*	
Journeys	Marie Thoger *Shanta*	Second
	Mary Cockett *Another Home Another Country*	
	Ian Serraillier *The Silver Sword*	
Friends and enemies: fans and gangs[1]	Stan Barstow *Joby*	Third
	Rosa Guy *The Friends*	
Survival	JV Marshall *Walkabout*	Fourth
	William Golding *Lord of the Flies*	
Minorities	Farrukh Dhondy *East End at Your Feet* (In conjunction with the four programme unit of the same title in Thames TV's English Programme and Longman's anthology *The Minority Experience*)	Fifth

'Home and school', 'Journeys', and 'Friends and enemies: fans and gangs' have all been particularly successful in this way. There is a plethora of material available for 'Home and school', and I have tended to devote the whole of the long autumn term to it. I found my original inspiration in the Penguin English Project's anthology *Family and School*; three novels featured there — Richard Wright's *Black Boy* (Longman), Camara Laye's *African Child* (Fontana) and Frederick Grice's *The Bonnie Pit Laddie* (OUP) — have since proved especially rich in resources. 'Journeys' can be used to incorporate a whole range of exciting and interesting experience — escapes; refugees; migration; transportation; and pilgrimages — and 'Friends and enemies; fans and gangs' has, in terms of children's writing, been the most productive of all, perhaps because of its proximity to their own lives.

Obviously enough, not all the 'lead' novels I have mentioned nor all the supplementary material deployed are in themselves multiracial; nor, for that matter, have all the themes I have experimented with lent themselves so readily to multiracialisation. 'Work' and 'Man and animals', both third year themes, have not, for example, and one very successful first and second year topic — the history of the school (1979 is its centenary year) based on the school log book — has been to all intents and purposes all-white. I do not think this matters. The idea of a multracial curriculum 'constant', propounded as part of the basic curriculum principle in the introduction, is slightly misleading; the 'constant' is certainly there in the books and materials available, and in the relationship between teachers and pupils (a point I return to later), but, as far as the 'manifest' curriculum set before children for them to engage with is concerned, it is more a question of establishing a curriculum 'regular' than a 'constant'.

Following a three year regimen of this sort it should be possible to make a more direct approach to the reality of multiracial Britain in the fourth and fifth. Others have worked with topics such as 'race relations', 'prejudice and discrimination' or 'oppression and liberation'; but, although I have certainly confronted the issue of racism in the classroom (through Farrukh Dhondy's stories — the outcome can be found in the final chapter), as a theme I have settled for 'Minorities', mainly because it is rather more likely to prove inclusive than exclusive. The original idea came from the ITV English programme which examined four different minorities — the unemployed, the deaf, the American Indian and migrant workers — and I was able to add from videotapes of earlier transmissions programmes on a mongol child, gypsies and Uganda Asians. Longman's accompanying anthology of prose, verse and photographs *The Minority Experience* offers much excellent supplementary material.

A more overt multiracial topic which foundered was 'Slavery', based on Paula Fox's *The Slave Dancer* (Piccolo) and excerpts from Author Haley's *Roots* (Hutchinson) and Julius Lester's *To Be a Slave* (Longman), which I attempted with the third year. In confining my selection of experience and material to the transatlantic slave trade, I erred on the side of exclusiveness. Either the same material should be included under a broader category, like 'Journeys', or 'Slavery' should be defined less restrictively so as to include slavery elsewhere and at other times. Some teachers have found it fruitful to make comparisons between the Afro-Caribbean experience, as reflected in novels such as *The Slave Dancer* and Morna Stuart's *Marassa and Midnight* (Heinemann), and the Romano-British experience, as reflected in novels like Henry Treece's *Legions of the Eagle* (Puffin) and Rosemary Sutcliff's *The Eagle of the Ninth* (OUP).

So much for the 'paper' curriculum. Time-consuming as its development may be, it is the implementation of such a curriculum in the classroom, what Douglas Barnes calls its 'enactment', which is truly problematic. It would take a successful enactment to involve the children wanting and being able to relate the curriculum's content to their own experience and aspirations. From a multiracial point of view, the signs of success are twofold — first, all pupils' acceptance that for the curriculum to draw on a diversity of racial and cultural sources is proper, normal and unremarkable; and, secondly, all pupils feeling secure enough in the classroom to want to share their racial and cultural experiences in talk and writing with myself and their peers.

The first sign is really a long-term aim, and one which so far has eluded me. Sometimes, indeed, the sheer weight of hostile white reaction, especially in the early days, felt very much like the reverse — abject failure, but it is possible that I somewhat misinterpreted the character of this response. It could be that it was more a rejection of me than the material, part of the business of trying out a new teacher, and in any case an inevitable stage white pupils adjusted to a predominantly white curriculum will have to pass through in readjusting to a multiracial one. However that may be, I defer a full discussion of hostile white reactions to the next chapter on books, because it has nearly always been particular books which have prompted them. As for the second sign of success, certain manifestations of that are almost as readily achieved as a change in the content of the stockcupboard — although sometimes the sharing may be confined to writing with the teacher as audience. The new generation of black children entering our secondary schools seem to me to feel much more confident and less ambiguous about themselves than their predecessors. As a result, race and culture enter naturally and readily into what they have to say and write. Writing about her best friend a first year black girl began, 'My friend Gemma is half the colour of me. Her dad is Jamaican and her mum is white....' One of the effects of reggae, Rastafarianism and the success of *Roots* has been that, for many black children, the old ambivalence over the African connexion has been replaced by a new romanticism. Consider this holiday advertisement by a second year black boy:

'Come to sweet Africa, Africa is a beautiful country. It is a West Indian country but people come to have their holiday there and enjoy theirself. The weather out there is always hot and there's plenty of fruit such as mango and breadfruit and sugar cane. The sea and the beach is a nice place to go with the palm trees as well. When you walk along the street you hear soul music and the reggae of Zion. And you also see the beautiful people.'

Or this by a third year black girl who has never visited the Caribbean:

'I would like to go to Jamaica for my honeymoon and I would like to go and visit people and get to know people who I don't know and I would like to pick mangoes and bananas. I would like to go on the beach and have a swim and see relatives over there.'

As readily tapped as black children's romantic sentiments towards Africa and the Caribbean is the nostalgia of Asian children who can recall memories of their family's country of origin or have visited it for a holiday. Yasmeen, a fifth form Muslim girl, wrote this piece of reminiscence about life in Kenya of her own accord as practice for the CSE essay:

The pleasures of being off sick

'Tahseen was really sick when we were in Kenya and she had to go to hospital for about 5 weeks. It cost us a fortune. Tahseen had kidney trouble and started getting blood in her urine. She was only about 6 and was terrified at the sight of blood. We got her to hospital and she stayed there for a few weeks. Dad gave about a pint of his blood to her and we went to see her when we could. Tahseen used to be on the ground floor and we could see her through the window. I remember this coloured man standing at the main door wouldn't let us in to see her because we were under age or something. We used to get really cross with him and at the same time beg him to let us see her for a few minutes. "No", he'd say "You're too small". Shaheen, me and Sayeed would go back to the car and wait for Mum and Dad to come back. Then one day the man at the door went in for a few minutes so we dashed for the main door and went to see Tahseen. Tahseen was happy to see us and after we told her what we had done she really laughed. Pity for us the man came in and told us we had to get out. So we did.

The next time we tried again to get in but failed, this time we had a wonderful idea and when the man was looking the other way, me, Shaheen and Sayeed knocked on Tahseen's window and when Mum opened it we all climbed in.

We'd never seen Tahseen so happy since she went away to hospital. Just then we heard the nurse outside so all of us made for the nearest place we could find. Two of us hid under the bed and Sayeed hid behind this screen. The nurse came, this tall broad lady at that, and tidied Tahseen's bed and gave her medicine. She was trying very hard not to laugh. A few minutes later she went away and we all chattered away about how we had tricked them all. About half an hour later we heard some body else behind the door. We didn't have time to get under the bed so one of us got in the cupboard and one under the trolley which had curtains round it and one behind the screen.

The door opened and the coloured man came in. He asked my father if he knew where we were, because he said he hadn't seen us and we weren't in the car. Dad looked at Tahseen and said quickly we might be playing some place. All right said the man and was about to go away when he turned around and made for the trolley. "Where are you taking that?" said Tahseen. "Back to the kitchen, looks like you finished." He was looking at the half empty plates on the trolley. "No, I haven't, I'm still hungry, very hungry," said Tahseen. The man looked at Tahseen and said, "All right", and went out closing the door behind him.

Sayeed came out from under the trolley and said that was close and that he was never going to hide there in a hurry.

We stayed there for about an hour eating all Tahseen's food, and playing with her, drinking her pop and everything. We climbed out of the window the same way we came in. Mum and Dad didn't come for a little while so we went to say hello to the man at the main door. He was really surprised because we had never greeted him like that before. We pretended that we wanted to get in so Shaheen and Sayeed looked at me and we nodded our heads and tried to run past him. He caught us though. We went back to the car and felt really happy.'

I mentioned in chapter 1 the self-confidence and pride increasingly to be found among Asian children. This is Shaheen, Yasmeen's younger sister, writing about parents and children:

'When I am a parent I would want to teach my children my culture and religion just as my parents teach me — to be able to teach them a culture so that they know they have a background and a sense of belonging. I am glad and proud to be a Muslim and I would very much like to know a lot more about my religion and I wish I could understand better. When my parents were at school they learnt their own language and I now regret that I don't know my language so well as it is part of my race and country. I would like to teach my children, if I have any, that they have got a race and they belong to it.'

White children too can be counted on to respond positively, but perfectly naturally, after regular exposure to multiracial innovations. A fourteen year old white girl wrote the following play 'Local Colour', inspired by a poem[2] of the same name describing a Glaswegian's somewhat ambiguous feelings about her Indian neighbour, as part of the 'Minorities' theme:

	'It was Monday morning about 9.30am. I'd just taken the kids to school and was thinking what I had to do when I got in. Something made me look up. I could see the woman from next door coming in my direction, would I say hello or just smile, she was getting nearer now and I decided I would say hello.'
Mrs. McDonald	'Hello' She looked at me and smiled. 'How are you finding Glasgow?' She looked a bit worried as if she didn't understand. She was silent for a short while then said:
Mrs. Kauzer	'It's allright'
Mrs. McDonald	'I expect you're finding it a bit cold.' She chuckled
Mrs. Kauzer	'Very'
Mrs. McDonald	'How is your husband?'
Mrs. Kauzer	'He is well thank you'
Mrs. McDonald	'Oh that's good'
Mrs. McDonald	'Would you like to come for a coffee a bit later?'
Mrs. Kauzer	'I have to go to the shop though.'
Mrs. McDonald	'Well maybe when you get back.' She smiled again.
Mrs. Kauzer	'That would be nice. I'm afraid my English isn't very good.'
Mrs. McDonald	'Oh I'll manage, anyway I think you're doing very well, a lot better than I would.'

Mrs. Kauzer	'I go to a class on a Wednesday night when I can for one hour to improve.'
Mrs. McDonald	'Why don't you go every Wednesday?'
Mrs. Kauzer	'Oh well, my husband is a bus driver you see and he has to do different, what do you call them?'
Mrs. McDonald	'Shifts'
Mrs. Kauzer	'Yes, shifts, and it means there's no one to look after the baby.'
Mrs. McDonald	'How old is he?'
Mrs. Kauzer	'10 months'
Mrs. McDonald	'When did you say it was? Every Wednesday night did you say.'
Mrs. Kauzer	'Yes'
Mrs. McDonald	'Well I don't do much on a Wednesday night after I've cooked the tea. So I wouldn't mind looking after him for you.'
Mrs. Kauzer	'Oh dear me, are you sure?'
Mrs. McDonald	'Of course I'm sure.'
Mrs. Kauzer	'Well it would only be on the Wednesday night when my husband is working.'
Mrs. McDonald	'Well we can talk about it a bit later, when you come for a cup of coffee o.k.'
Mrs. Kauzer	'O.k., what does o.k. mean?'
Mrs. McDonald	'Oh its just a saying we use, instead of having to say all right.'
Mrs. Kauzer	'Oh well, o.k. then.'
Mrs. McDonald	'See you later.'
Mrs. Kauzer	'Yes. See you later.'

It is predictable that children will respond to a multiracial input with writing out of their own racial and cultural experience. When the same sort of response is stimulated by inputs of a non-multiracial kind, it would be justifiable to claim a major breakthrough. A black third year girl, after reading a South African story called 'Power' about a swallow trapped by an overhead power line, wrote a story of her own called 'Trapped' which described the capture of an African villager by white slavers and his transportation to the West Indies.

Even more remarkable was a story written by a third year Sikh girl, Baljit, who was notorious in the school for skipping off lessons and swearing at teachers. As part of the theme on 'Work' we had been reading Martin Ballard's novel *Dockie* (Lions) in class. Set in the East End dockland in the 1920s it is, like Frederick Grice's *The*

Bonnie Pit Laddie, refreshingly authentic in its treatment of working-class life. Moggy, the hero, leaves school at 14 for a seemingly inevitable career in the insecure world of casual dock labour but determined to extricate himself by making his way as a boxer. There is a strike at the docks. Whereas Moggy goes on the picket line, his father, also a docker, decides he has to keep working in order to pay the midwife for the delivery of his wife's new baby. As a result 'Scab' is painted in big letters across the front of his house and Moggy's younger brother is beaten up at school. We had a heated discussion in class on the rights and wrongs of the different decisions taken, and someone raised the possibility of a school strike. A fortnight later it actually happened (this was in March 1978). Most of the school walked out and refused to do any work for an afternoon because the teachers' industrial action had deprived them of their dinners. Baljit had ideas of her own about what might cause a school strike. This was the story she wrote:

The Punjabi Gang

'The school was on strike because of colour differences. In this school there was only about 350 kids. There was 200 Punjabi people in this school and about 150 black people. And then after a time more white people came, about 100 of them*. Nearly every Punjabi boy wore a turban on his head and nearly all the girls wore trousers. Everybody picked on brown people just because they were different religioned and wore different clothes. And everybody said, "Pakis out", because we speaked in our own language. I really got fed up and I said to every Punjabi people in school that don't come to school on the following day. On the next day there wasn't no Punjabi people in school. There was only white people and black and the teachers got shocked about this. On that day the teachers tried to go round everybody houses who was away, but they couldn't because there was so many. But Mr. R.T. (name of the third year tutor) knew that I was the leader of the gang so he came round to my house. And he said to me, "Tell all the gang to come back to school", but I said, "NO! NO! NO! and that's that". But Mr. T kept on saying, "If anybody say anything else you come and tell me and I'll do something about it." So I said, "Okay". So I told all my gang to come back to

---

*In fact about two thirds of the children in the school were white. The main minority were Punjabi-speaking Muslims. The number of Sikh children could be counted on the fingers of one hand.

school. When we was in school nobody said a word about it. This time the Punjabi people start saying to white people, "White honkeys and bloody white shit." No one said nothing so I think the Punjabi people won. HA! HA! HA!'
Finish'

It is a fine story, bold and entertaining — a judgement I naturally passed on to Baljit; it is also a vigorous piece of racial self-assertion (the wearing of traditional dress, the use of the mother tongue, anti-white abuse), although Baljit was very quick to tell me during our discussion of her story that most of her friends were white, a fact I had already been aware of. However, I do not think it would be unfair to say that in all the British staff rooms I have known Baljit's story would have been poorly received (to put it mildly) by the overwhelming majority of teachers. In one or two it would have been regarded as a suitable case for disciplinary action. The extent to which this claim is sound, the extent to which Baljit's story is unacceptable, represents the extent to which the teaching profession has failed to respond adequately to the challenge of teaching in multiracial Britain.

I want to use Baljit's story to introduce a fuller discussion of language, not bilingualism or teaching English as a second language (which lie outside the confines of the brief I have set myself), but the question of attitudes to language, particularly attitudes to linguistic correctness and non-standard dialects.

In my first term at the school I attempted a rough and ready analysis of the kind which, I argued at the end of chapter 1, should be integral to curriculum planning. I identified in my pupils three classically interrelated symptoms of an inner-city malady which made for a frustrating time in the classroom for teacher and learner alike — poor standards of attainment in reading and writing, lack of motivation and low self-esteem. I took the last named to be crucial. Many black and white (but not Asian) children seemed to be arriving at secondary school believing, tacitly rather than openly, that they came from 'bad' homes, lived in a 'bad' area and went to a 'bad' school ('a dump', as one child introduced it to me in the week of my arrival). Of special relevance from my point of view, within this general sense of inadequacy, was the conviction, widespread among both black and white mother tongue speakers of English, that their version of it was 'poor' 'ungrammatical' 'not proper' and so on. As an illustration I offer an extract from an essay by Shirley, a fifth year black girl and herself an immigrant from the Caribbean:

'The West Indian people talk English but in a bad way ... I remember when I first came up here I couldn't speak the language properly and used to talk the same bad language as I used to talk in the West Indies. They used to keep asking me what I said or if they did understand laughed at me. But I came to school every day, done English even done English homework and now I speak English as good as anybody who was here long time before me.'*

On this model the mother tongue is not conceived of as an acquisition to cherish, a point for growth, for extension into a wider repertoire of linguistic accomplishment; instead, it becomes an inheritance of doubtful value, to be replaced perhaps by a 'superior' version, and a poor preparation certainly for what come to seem society's intimidating linguistic demands. The chances of securing an about-face are slim. Generations of indoctrination as to what should count as 'good' or 'correct' English are against it; resistance is deeply entrenched not only in the teaching profession but among parents and society at large as well. What hope is there for the Shirleys of Britain when the headmaster of an 80% black London comprehensive school can say, 'Should I put Creole on the timetable? Over my dead body, and the majority of my parents would cheer me to the skies. They want their children to get jobs. I will not even allow *patois* plays in the school. It must not be elevated to linguistic status at the expense of English' (*Sunday Times*, 16th October 1977).

Just how deeply entrenched such attitudes are was brought home to me by a difference of opinion between myself and the West Midlands Examinations Board over the oral component in the CSE exam. The instructions for the marking of the conversation test appeared to me to imply that only speakers of Standard English could score full marks. I queried whether this was so at a moderation meeting and, being told that it was, wrote a letter of complaint to the secretary of the board, pointing out that it made no sense linguistically and amounted to social class prejudice. Part of the reply I received from the assistant secretary reads:

*I am conscious of appearing to contradict myself by claiming to have detected in minority race children *both* increased self-confidence *and* continuing self-doubt. In fact there is no contradiction. The two phenomena are simply paradoxical facets of a complicated truth. Sometimes, of course, as with white children, vigorous self-assertion in the classroom may be a defence against self-hate.

'I think the first point to make is that in both Reading Aloud and Conversation the Panel has always stressed that no candidate should be penalised for a local accent unless it interferes with communication. Your letter, however, refers to the candidates' dialect which is rather different. The point here is that as this is an examination in English Language, the Board could not possibly justify awarding full marks for a candidate who says "writ" for "wrote", "done" for "did" to quote a few examples in your letter. However, because a candidate does not obtain full marks does not mean he is necessarily excluded from Grade 1. The Notes of Guidance for the Oral Examination state that the comments about each mark category are applicable to the highest mark in each grade. This means that a candidate with excellent material and initiative and good vocabulary and idiom etc., could lose a mark or two for errors in grammar and pronunciation but still could come within the Grade 1 category.

The same principle applies in the written papers. A candidate writing non-standard English, which included spelling and grammatical errors, could not expect to gain full marks but provided that his material, arrangement of ideas, expression etc., were to the required standard, there would be no reason why he should not achieve a Grade 1.'

It may only be a matter of a few marks, but there are clear issues of fact and principle at stake. The assistant secretary seems to be under the misapprehension that the verb forms I quoted — 'writ' and 'done' — are mistakes, as though the children who say or write them have mislearned something. If we return to Baljit's story we can find grammatical mistakes — 'we speaked', 'everybody houses' — which are due, obviously enough, to her not being a mother tongue speaker of English, but other of her usages, which I imagine the assistant secretary would want to call 'errors' — 'we was', 'No one said nothing', etc, are perfectly regular features of local grammar and in no proper sense of the word mistakes.

I contented myself with the hope that English panel, to whom the assistant secretary had promised to refer the matter, might enlighten him. Far from it; he wrote again shortly afterwards to say the panel fully supported his position and had nothing to add to his earlier letter; which convinced me, if I needed convincing, that a basic course in linguistics should be a mandatory element in the training of all English teachers. However, there was a happy ending of a kind to this story. I managed to find a like-minded head of

English for the usual pairing arrangement in the oral examination. We both taught in working-class schools, which meant that all the mother tongue speakers among our pupils spoke a non-standard form of English, and agreed that, since the board's direction on non-standard dialects was poppycock, we would flout it. We awarded three of his candidates who gave outstanding accounts of themselves in the conversation test full marks.

Concern over the denigration of non-standard dialect explains the inclusion of the two knowledge objectives and the first affective objective in the list at the beginning of the chapter, and the emphasis given to them in my teaching. How are they to be realised? Not easily, that is for sure. I adopt two strategies. The first is a straightforward curriculum unit about language of the sort many teachers have experimented with. It includes information on the languages of the world, the history of English, and dialect and accent. I pay particular attention to explaining the origins of and need for a standard dialect and the grammatical and lexical differences between that standard and Jamaican Creole on the one hand and Birmingham dialect on the other. Appreciating this material is well within the competence of first years. I repeat it with older pupils adding further items on style, register and that most important of concepts 'appropriateness'. The trouble with 'appropriateness' is that it has become something of a word to conjure with. Teachers often say that, although non-standard grammar may be technically 'correct', it is not 'appropriate' for writing. But, whilst 'correctness' is a pretty fixed category, 'appropriateness' is open to negotiation and revision. Many teachers would regard Baljit's use of language in her story as inappropriate for an English exercise book. She obviously would not, nor would I. In teaching children, for example, that certain kinds of language are appropriate for CSE essays and job applications and others not, one should also be teaching them that it is because examiners and employers hold the power to define the terms.

It is important that this first strategy should involve the pupils themselves in a discussion of language use and social attitudes. I have found extracts from two novels fruitful with first and second years. Mary Cockett's *Another Home Another Country* (Chatto, Boyd and Oliver) is a popular multiracial story with younger pupils, although I find its presentation of black experience distinctly ambivalent. The relevant moment is when Luke, a recent arrival from Jamaica, uses dialect at news time in class, 'Yesterday I go to do park, and I play wid de baby', whereupon he is 'corrected' by his teacher and made to practise 'th' sounds in public. The teacher's conduct is, of course, iniquitous, but there is nothing to indicate that the author thinks so. I asked for comments from my second year group. They were deeply divided, the black children as much as the white, but the majority view was that she had been perfectly justified — 'he is in England and should learn the English way of speech', 'teachers have to correct children who say words the wrong way'.

A girl of Irish parentage who had been moved to tears at one point in the narrative thought it smart to make a joke out of the dialect episode in her written critique — 'I tink dat de teacher was right to correct Luke because otherwise she might have dem all speak like dat'. It is ironical that an Irish child should choose to make a joke out of it, since 't' for 'th' is also a feature of the Irish accent, which is the occasion for the drama in the second extract — from Bill Naughton's autobiographical novel *One Small Boy* (Longman) set in Lancashire in the 1920s. M'Cloud, the small boy, says 'ting' instead of 'thing' during a poetry recitation lesson. After several failures his teacher, Miss Skegham, snaps, 'Don't you know the King's English yet, M'Cloud?' Whereupon the boy reflects, 'King's English — I'm Irish. She's saying that against the Irish', and he clams up, refusing to recite another word. Through the savage beating he receives he thinks of the Irish hero Robert Emmet; eventually, forced to kneel until he obeys, he passes out. Naturally the children reading this extract were more indignant about the teacher's conduct than they were about the conduct of Luke's teacher. Karen, a third year white girl, wrote:

> 'I think Michael is doing the right thing standing up for what he believes just like Robert Emmet did, and Miss Skegham, well I thought she was being a bit unreasonable with him. It should have occurred to her that he wouldn't be able to say "thing" if he was Irish. I don't think she understood why Michael was acting stubborn. She probably didn't realise that she hurt his feelings when she said, "Don't you know the King's English yet?" '

Sadly there are still many Miss Skeghams in schools up and down the country needlessly creating anxieties about language — 'correcting' accent and grammar and offering a host of unwarranted prescriptions about not starting sentences with 'and' and 'because' and so forth.

The second strategy is to give children every encouragement to use their natural speech, not only in talk and drama, but in personal writing and stories as well. In a way white children need more support here than black children because, although the latter would never probably claim that Creole was linguistically as good as standard English (which is, of course, precisely what it is), it does have glamour and style and they will cherish it in the way that all children will cherish a private argot that has status in the peer group. Nowadays, if I ask a first year group who speaks a language other than English, the black hands will go up as quickly as the brown ones and someone can be counted on to say with a grin, 'Jamaican'. They will respond with pleasure to any examples of Creole writing put before them, Linton Kwesi Johnson's poems *Dread Beat and Blood* (Bogle L'Ouverture) being a notable favourite, and quickly have a go at their own.

They have also developed, quite naturally, considerable facility in moving between Creole and the local form of British English. Once I observed two second year girls during drama doing a shopping scene together in a Creole I could not understand. I asked them to show it to the rest of the class. 'We'll do it in English', one said. 'No,' I said, 'The way you did it.' They did it in Creole, but in a Creole skilfully adjusted so that everyone in the room could follow. I should perhaps add that once or twice I have been rebuffed for seeming to threaten Creole's value for black children as a secret code. After I had been more than usually inquisitive about the meaning of certain phrases, a black girl in my tutor group wrote on the board, 'Sir is nosey about black people's language.'

It is unfortunate that the initiatives taken by many teachers to rehabilitate non-standard dialect[3] should have been interpreted, in the manner of the headteacher quoted above, to be 'at the expense' of standard English. It goes without saying that one of the school's tasks is to help children master the reading and writing of standard English (to aim for anything less would be irresponsible), but the path to this goal, it must be stressed, does not lie through the deprecation of non-standard forms of the mother tongue. The two aims ought to be mutually supportive — both indispensable to the realisation of full mother tongue competence.

In attempting to multracialise an English curriculum, I am not conscious of having undertaken anything remarkable or revolutionary. It seemed an obvious development at the time, part of a more general process of rectification in the choice of curriculum content which, notably, also involved changes in the presentation of sex roles and working-class experience. In the same city I have come across other teachers of English who have done similar things (in several cases made far greater use of Afro-Caribbean literature than I have), without imagining they were doing anything out of the ordinary, as natural responses to the situations confronting them.

If there is a curriculum 'constant' it resides not so much in the content of the 'manifest' curriculum as in the relationships between teacher and learners (and the secondary relationships between learners and learners they help to create) without which almost nothing could be achieved. Unfortunately I cannot boast of having achieved the kind of relationships established by the teacher whose work was featured in the previous chapter, but just once or twice moments of intercultural communication have been fashioned, as if out of nowhere, to serve as timely reminders of what is possible and restore my flagging faith.

For instance, the fifth year and I had been watching the ITV English programme on sex roles (part of the 'Viewpoints' unit on the media). At the end Barry, whose portrait is depicted in the final chapter, took charge of discussion, relegating me to a back seat, because he had been angered by what he saw as the programme's bias. He challenged any girl to say that she was dissatisfied with her lot. None did. What those who spoke up had to say reflected a model of future happiness lifted wholesale and uncritically from precisely the sources the programme had been attacking. One often argumentative and obstreperous girl said she liked being 'ordered about' by her boyfriend. Suddenly one of Barry's cronies turned to the Asian girls, who had been quiet up to then, and said, 'You even have your husbands picked for you.' 'That's not true,' retorted Rashida, 'Not picked', and she explained exactly what an arranged marriage in the Muslim community involved. 'You have the right to say no', she insisted. 'What about if you wanted to marry a white boy?' someone asked. 'Oh no,' said Rashida with a smile, 'That would be out of the question — for most families anyway. Unless he changed his religion, of course.'

Similar areas of dialogue, virgin territory as far as the classroom was concerned, were opened up later by some of the stories in Farrukh Dhondy's *East End at Your Feet*. I do not think it is an exaggeration to maintain that children derive more from (certainly set greater store by) the way their teachers behave towards them (and the effect this has on the way their peers behave towards them) than from the ideas, facts and materials which they are asked to engage with in the 'manifest' curriculum. Possibly the comparison should not be made for, if we can say that teachers' behaviour is part of the 'real' curriculum, we can also say that the 'manifest' curriculum is part of teachers' behaviour.

References

1   'Borrowed' from Judith Atkinson's article in *Teaching English Across the Ability Range* (Ward Lock).
2   'Local colour' by Liz Lockhead *The Minority Experience* (Longman) p 112.
3   Some of those undertaken with West Indian children primarily in mind can be found summarised in Viv Edwards's *The West Indian Language Issue in British Schools* (Routledge).

5   Books in the Multiracial Classroom

'It is strange, is it not, how sometimes a soul will speak to a soul across language, across the generations, across every difference of race and birth and breeding.'
Neena in Peter Dickinson's *The Devils' Children*

'I don't want to read about coloureds.'
14 year old white girl

One of my preoccupations on the Schools Council project was with the evaluation of books and materials from a multiracial point of view. My assessment was that, although a good deal had been achieved in the way of annotated lists of recommended books and critiques of racial bias and stereotyping, both lists and critiques had fallen short by and large in not making explicit the criteria underpinning their judgments or in couching them in terms too general to be operational. I felt that, if the selection of teaching materials was to become more consistent and effective, it was to the definition of precise, operational criteria (of the level of specificity already to be found in American guidelines) that attention should now be directed. The outcome of this conviction was the set of criteria quoted in chapter 2.

I have commented in the previous chapter on how comparatively easy I found it, armed with the project experience (among other factors), to start multiracialising the content of the English stock cupboard and the shelves of the school library. I was able to introduce the class readers mentioned in the previous chapter; to make available for individual reading just about all the other multiracial fiction in print for the age range 11-16 that I was familiar with (there are genuine difficulties involved in books being out of print and in keeping up to date); and to begin a new library section for books written in Gujerati, Hindi, Punjabi and Urdu.

Multiracialising stock cupboards and libraries also, of course, means withdrawing from circulation what is inaccurate or inappropriate. Project experience had taught me that many books in regular school use, and indeed currently available on publishers' lists (at any rate between 1973 and 1975), were either blatantly racist or more subtly biased; and that particular vigilance needed to be exerted over out-of-date text books, stereotypic topic books and children's fiction written in the colonial era. Books I have withdrawn fall into all three categories, and they confirm the project's general conclusion that of all the cultures and races misrepresented by British books for children over the years it is Africa and black people that have been most persistently caricatured and maligned.

The first offender to lose its place on the library shelves was a large and garish *Illustrated Book About Africa* (so battered I could find no trace of publisher or publication date, only the year of accession — 1966) which included, among many passages of misinformation, the following:

'To the white settlers of East Africa, the Kikuyu have been the most helpful — and at times the most troublesome — of all the native tribes … For the most part, they have been faithful and competent workers in the factories and fields. From time to time, secret societies aimed at overthrowing British rule have sprung up among the Kikuyu tribesmen. The most recent of these was the Mau Mau revolt, led by fanatic religious and political leaders. In this rebellion, a great many Englishmen were brutally murdered — along with thousands of Kikuyu who had remained loyal to the Europeans — before the uprising was finally put down and the leaders imprisoned or driven out of the country.'

The last sentence is a classic of its kind. For the benefits of those unfamiliar with these tragic years of Kenyan history, the 'great many Englishmen', including servicemen, who died during the Mau Mau emergency (and who merit a main clause rather than the parenthesis the 'thousands of Kikuyu' have to settle for) numbered less than 100. It is instructive to compare this passage with one from a new textbook, 'an introduction to the history of the Africans', *Discovering Africa's Past* (Longman), by the distinguished historian Basil Davidson.

'Elsewhere the local white settler communities strongly opposed any political advance for Africans. The opposition was toughest of all in Kenya. Only a great African farmers' rebellion there, the so called "Mau Mau" of the middle 1950s, in which some 10,000 Africans lost their lives in fighting against the British army and white-settler soldiers, was able to open the gate to African independence.' (pp 203/204)

This is certainly a different version of the same events but not, in my view, much of an improvement. If the first's emphasis on the defeat of Mau Mau seems to find no place (implicitly) for the murders at Hola camp, then neither does the second's on 'a great African farmers' rebellion' for the massacre at Lari. It might be argued, in the latter's defence, that a 200 page overview for school pupils of the whole continent's history cannot possibly encompass all the necessary qualifications in writing about a decade in the life of one country. In which case, why write it? Anyway Davidson's version seems to me almost as biased as the first and certainly something pupils need to be fortified against.

Shortly afterwards clearing out the English stock cupboard I unearthed a set of guides to letter writing (published by Wheaton in 1958). Its specimen letter from abroad was written in immaculate copperplate by Cecil John Kinley of the David Livingstone School for Boys in Bulawayo to his friend Tom in England. Part of his letter reads:

> 'I live with my mother and father in a rather nice bungalow out-side Bulawayo. My father is manager in the Iron and Steel Works there. We have two native servants to see to all the housework. We call them "Boys" although they are both nearly thirty. One of them named Sixpence looks after my black pony Lobengula. Today Sixpence jumped over the stable door and ran away when I suddenly showed him my chameleon. The natives think that chameleons are the spirits of the dead.'

From the fiction section of the library I have removed a number of novels of the Biggles ilk — amongst them *Flame over Africa* by Eric Leyland (published by Hodder and Stoughton in 1951 and accessed in 1965). David Flame and friends are hired by the Foreign Office to investigate Communist-inspired trouble brewing in a British African dependency ('stealthy evil was afoot in the jungle'). At the centre of it is Ch'aka, the 'fat, venomously ugly' chief of the Greater Kombolo, who is suborned by Communist agents posing as mission-aries (suspect from the start because none of them are English — 'all foreigners, Greeks and Rumanians') into inciting his people to an atavistic uprising (which reminds David of 'the Nazi lunacy at the Nuremberg rallies') designed to drive the white oppressors into the sea. Fortunately for the latter the loyal and civilised N'goni are at hand to save them led by their chief Kachaje who was educated at an English public school — where he was called 'Sambo' and 'so popular, for there had been no colour bar there'.

As if the narrative were not bad enough, the novel's pages are peppered with demeaning observations and asides:

'These [natives], though they gave off an odour which Tony did not find very pleasant, had been useful, to say the least.'

'It had been proved that to teach the savage to use weapons of destruction was something like a million times easier than to teach him the arts of peace and civilization.'

'Some [chiefs] had achieved this ambition [to own a car] though it was usual for them to harness oxen to it when they discovered just how expensive was petrol.'

Such books are easy targets and can be disposed of without qualms — provided it is clear that the grounds for withdrawal are that they are racially or culturally libellous (both inaccurate and insulting). It is perhaps worth adding that some teachers have found it possible to make constructive critical use of them in the classroom, and also that diplomatically speaking, bearing headteachers in mind, replacement is preferable to withdrawal. I was, for instance, pleased to be able to substitute for the *Illustrated Book About Africa* Macdonald's excellent *Encyclopedia of Africa* which won the Times Educational Supplement's Information Book Award in 1976.

As a teacher for the past two years my concern has been more with use than choice — how best to negotiate the problems presented by adverse white reactions and, more generally, how to extract maximum benefit from the introduction of multiracial literature in the classroom. The first, and distinctly intractable, problem was posed by the traditional ingredients of the CSE literature course, some of which I inherited from my predecessors and some of which I installed myself. I am thinking specifically of three English books — William Golding's *Lord of the Flies*, Peter Terson's *Zigger-Zagger*, Shelagh Delaney's *A Taste of Honey* — and three American ones — Mark Twain's *Tom Sawyer*, John Steinbeck's *Of Mice and Men* and Arthur Miller's *The Crucible*. I do not wish to dissociate myself now from the selection of these books. I would use all of them again gladly. None of them are in any sense racist, but they do all (with the exception perhaps of *A Taste of Honey*) either describe racist situations or include racist references.

The three American books are set in slave-owning or segregationist contexts. Blacks are shadowy background figures in *Tom Sawyer* and, although 'white, mulatto and negro' children play together happily enough, it is only too apparent that white society consigns them to separate and unequal destinies. At one point Injun Joe is moved to complain that a justice of the peace had him 'horse-whipped in front of the jail, like a nigger.' The only black character

in *The Crucible*, a play set in a seventeenth century Puritan community, is Tituba, a slave from Barbados. She is sympathetically
presented but shown to be superstitious and gullible as well, and
when Abigail is asked by her uncle Parris why no family in the
village will employ her as a servant, she retorts haughtily, 'They
want slaves, not such as I. Let them send to Barbados for that. I will
not black my face for any of them.' There is only one black too in
Of Mice and Men, a novel set in California in the thirties — Crooks,
the crippled stable buck. He lives on his own in the harness room,
not with the white ranch hands in the bunkhouse. His response to
segregation is a posture of aloof pride, what Steinbeck calls 'the
terrible protective dignity of the negro'.

Within the confines of the novel it is a sympathetic portrait, as is
the portrait of the black boyfriend in *A Taste of Honey* but the
latter never develops (unlike Crooks) beyond a vague sketch, a
generalised notion of a person — a striking failure in a play
distinguished by its characterisation. Even less convincing is the
appearance made by black people (bus conductor and passengers)
in one scene of *Zigger-Zagger*; they are introduced simply to
illustrate the hooliganism of football fans (admittedly they do
emerge as victors from the racial slanging-match). The essential
point is that an unrelieved regimen of such portraits, however
sympathetic in themselves, can only amount in the eyes of a
contemporary child, deprived of the necessary social or historical
understanding, to a kind of unitary characterisation of the black
man or woman as inferior — slave, menial, walk-on actor, problem.

There is no doubt that this sort of fiction and drama can present
difficulties in multiracial classrooms — sometimes even irresolvable
ones, since almost too much has to be explained and understood. I
described in chapter 1 an incident arising out of the use of 'niggers'
in *Lord of the Flies* which I might have anticipated, but failed to
handle adequately. Some critics of racism in books have argued,
partly on the basis of this kind of incident, that such books should
either not be used in the classroom at all or at least be presented in a
properly censorious manner. One critic in an issue of London
NAME's broadsheet *Issues in Race and Education* (April/May
1976) took Golding to task for the 'niggers' episode and also in
general for giving currency to stereotypes about savagery in his
description of Jack and his tribe's wilful descent into barbarism.
Manifestly this is to misread the novel, to ignore the intended
relationship with *Coral Island*, and to confound an author with his
characters. I am afraid it is typical of the simple-minded nonsense
critiques of 'racist' literature so often degenerate into.

For me there is no question of not using *Lord of the Flies* nor of shirking any awkward confrontations which reading it might generate. It is a matter of developing the self-confidence to handle these situations productively. Reading *A Taste of Honey* with one fifth year group yielded an interesting, if not exactly productive, discussion. No one made any comment on the black boyfriend nor on the mixed race baby whose arrival is imminent as the play closes. But the boys reacted virulently against the homosexual character who is so warmly delineated; to such an extent that not one of them would read his part (I had to read it). I told them they were being absurdly prejudiced, and one or two of the girls rounded on them too. But there was no shifting them. As far as they were concerned he was a 'poofter' and that was that.

That sexual stereotypes might be more firmly ensconced than racial ones I also found when reading *The Devil's Children* with a first year group (not the same group who figure in the assessment of the novel later in the chapter). I drew their attention to the fact that the main character, a girl, was active and resourceful in a way often reserved for boys in children's fiction. The boys were sceptical, even dismissive — she was only a 'tomboy', and anyway girls never displayed such qualities 'in real life'; this, in defiance of the presence in their class of at least two 'real life' equivalents.

The main answer, of course, to difficult classroom experiences with traditional CSE literature, is to make available throughout the five years of compulsory secondary schooling a more varied and balanced reading programme in which black people feature prominently and positively. Not that this would betoken the end of uncomfortable responses. Possibly quite the reverse. Those teachers who argue against multiracialising the curriculum because it will 'stir things up' are right in one sense. It will, at least in multiracial secondary schools, but stirring up is exactly what is so desperately needed.

J.V. Marshall's *Walkabout* is one novel I introduced to rectify the racial balance in the CSE literature course which almost foundered because of adverse reactions from white pupils. Some of the fourth year group I read it with last year found confirmation of their prejudices in the first fifty pages. The young white boy, Peter, addresses the Aborigine as 'Darkie', whilst his older sister's fear of the latter's nakedness reflects the values of her upbringing in the southern states of America. When he attempts to touch her out of pure curiosity (never having seen white people before), Mary is petrified:

'The idea of being manhandled by a naked black boy appalled her: struck at the root of one of the basic principles of her civilized code. It was terrifying; revolting; obscene. Back in Charleston it would have got the darkie lynched.'

Both Peter's language and Mary's revulsion were greeted with laughter and facetious comments by white pupils, and there was some insistence that a black boy, the class buffoon, should read the part of the Aborigine even though the author is at pains to emphasise that his blackness was different from an African's. Patently the author's object is to dispel stereotypes, raise questions about the application of 'primitive' and 'civilized' and celebrate intercultural communication, but appreciating that necessitates finishing the book and finishing any book was a major ordeal, attitudinally rather than technically, for most of the class. What saved the novel, and its message, was the timely showing on television of Nicholas Roeg's visually stunning film version which, usefully enough, has a good deal to add about the white man's exploitation of the black.

Evaluating how successful books have been is an essential part of using them, but also a difficult one since reading for children is normally, as it is for adults, a private activity. Such response as they do make is often minimal or hard to interpret. The obvious exception is the unmistakeable pleasure displayed by minority race children, whether aged five or fifteen, at encountering books including people like themselves. 'Have you got any West Indian books, Sir?' or 'Have you got any books about black people?' have been commonplace questions in the library. Linton Kwesi Johnson's *Dread Beat and Blood*, Rosa Guy's *The Friends*, Farrukh Dhondy's *East End at Your Feet*, Bernard Ashley's *The Trouble With Donovan Croft* and Julius Lester's *To Be a Slave* are some of the books which have been enthusiastically received.

I have also had one instance of black rejection — of Paula Fox's novel about slavery *The Slave Dancer*, a novel, it will be remembered, used successfully (albeit in excerpts) by the teacher in chapter 3. It is a noble book, in my judgement, finely written, exciting and harrowing — sparing children none of the grim details of enslavement and the slave ships. The degeneration of the white crew is vividly evoked, and attention drawn to the inevitable implication of the innocent like the hero, the white boy Jessie, who was pressganged by the slavers to play his pipe during the slaves' exercise on deck. He discovers as an adult the impossibility of avoiding the taint, no matter what his personal convictions, by virtue of his mere existence in a society that condones slavery and the maltreatment of blacks. Moreover, it is not only enslaved or demoralised blacks who appear. Jessie and Ras, the boy slave he befriends, are saved after the shipwreck by an escaped slave, who behaves with quiet dignity and directs them on their respective roads to freedom.

But appreciating all this meant, as with *Walkabout*, finishing the book, and several black children in the third year class I tried it with had decided they had had enough after forty pages, partly (it seemed) because of the slaves' racist language, which had left the second year in chapter 2 unmoved, and partly because of the degradation of the slaves' life on board. 'It gives offence', they said, and one girl of Indian/white parentage added, 'It's embarrassing, sir. You see I've got a black dad and a white mum. It's like when the National Front or Mrs. Thatcher comes on the television.' I took a vote, and it was overwhelmingly carried that the reading of the novel should stop forthwith. Ironically I had chosen to try it out on this class before any other because they enjoyed reading a story together and because I was confident about my relationship with them. The term before Rosa Guy's novel *The Friends* had been a popular choice, especially with the girls; and yet the main character Phyllisia, a West Indian girl who goes to join her father in New York, is on the receiving end of far more virulent abuse from her black American classmates (of the 'Go back and swing in the trees' variety) than the slaves from the slavers in *The Slave Dancer*. At the end of *The Friends* a white girl asked a question I have never been asked by any other white child, 'Sir, have you got any more books about coloured people?' (I gave her Jean McGibbon's *Hal* (Heinemann) which she liked too.)

Most of the spontaneous responses made by white children have been negative. A white fourteen year old was quick to interrupt a discussion of 'The Rivers of Babylon', the popular reggae song, with the observation that my introducing it was 'an imposition on white people'; a twelve year old girl criticised *The Young Warriors* for having neither girls nor whites in it (not strictly true, of course); and a third year boy picked up Madeleine Blakeley's *Nahda's Family* (A & C Black) off my desk and said with a grin, 'God, they're getting everywhere — even into books now'. The most serious episode involved the vandalising of a play about Martin Luther King — Colin Hodgetts' *We Will Suffer and Die If We Have To* (Religious Education Press). During a routine library check I found that its inside cover had been inscribed with racist graffiti — 'Enoch rules OK', 'Enoch rules over Luther King', 'Up the Third Reich', 'Hitler is OK', 'Whites rule Pakis OK', 'Wogs are *slaves* to white people'.

In the early days negative white responses preoccupied me constantly, although they were confined to a minority of children. I neither knew what to make of them, whether expressed earnestly or light-heartedly, nor what to do about them. Of only one thing was I certain — that, oddly enough, I did not really wish to inhibit them. Now I think I would distinguish what are obviously meant as jokes, such as those quoted at the end of chapter 1, from what are obviously meant to hurt or be offensive. Jokes are an important element in clasroom and playground culture; in secondary schools racial ones are often given and taken in good part. Teachers who assume a high moral tone are opening themselves to ridicule. If the joke is funny, it makes better sense to laugh, as I did over the 'Bangladesh gentleman' quip quoted in chapter 1.

Deliberately malicious gibes or graffiti are another matter; although I would want to make a distinction between those whose target was other children and those whose target was in fact (whatever it might be ostensibly) myself. The former, especially (it goes without saying) racial taunting or bullying, demand the full weight of the school's disciplinary apparatus. In the case of the latter it is probably sounder tactics to play it cool. I return to the question of more deeply intended expressions of white racism in the next chapter.

More detailed evaluation of the effectiveness of different books means more intensive use, more teaching, that is, and more active pupil participation in the shape of stories, poems, drama and discussion. My only major evaluation[1] to date has been of Peter Dickinson's *The Devil's Children* which I read as a class novel with a first year group. I was considerably helped by the presence of an evaluator in the classroom; experiencing from the other side the benefits of the kind of curriculum research exemplified in chapter 3. I chose this particular novel because it was widely praised on publication in the late sixties, for, among other things, a highly respectful portrait of a British cultural minority, the Sikh community, and because in spite of this I knew of no teacher who had used it in the classroom. The choice of class was equally calculated. Its ethnic composition was typical of the school — a white majority (most of whom were Irish or half Irish), four Pakistanis, two Sikhs, two of mixed parentage (one Irish/Indian, the other English/ Yemeni), and one Jamaican. Its ethos was less typical. Interracial harmony was the dominant norm, with strong interracial friendships and separate cultural identities masked or understated, the product, perhaps, of that most insidious of primary school philosophies, 'children are just children'.

Classically evaluation purports to match outcomes with objectives. This was not the sort of evaluation I or the evaluator was concerned with. I did not have objectives of the traditional kind. On the Schools Council Project I believed that fiction could be used to promote the overriding multiracial objectives of respect for self and respect for others, but I have been unable to square this approach either with the way I want to teach English or with the classroom relationships I want to foster. So, to revert to the terminology of chapter 2, I settled for an 'expressive' rather than an 'instructional' aim. I was just interested to see what a happily integrated class, including two Sikh girls, would make of such an overtly multiracial novel as *The Devil's Children*.

They were exposed to it over a period of a month. I divided the novel into four sections and each week allotted an hour's lesson to the exploration of a section's issues through discussion and drama. Discussion involved answering questions, some comprehension and others open-ended, and the children could choose to work individually, in pairs or in groups. A different group taped its own deliberations each week. For drama the groups (not the same as for discussion, since I insisted on mixing the sexes) were asked to work on what seemed to me an important episode in the section and, if they wished, they could show the result to the rest of the class. At the end of the month a Sikh student teacher came to answer their questions on Sikhism; and finally, by way of summative evaluation, they wrote stories (carrying on where Dickinson leaves off), completed questionnaires inviting their opinions and were interviewed, singly or in pairs, by the evaluator.

The novel is about prejudice and hostility towards what is unfamiliar — but at the same time removed from the realities of contemporary racism by its futuristic setting. Its message is as transparent as (and almost identical to) *Walkabout's*; it is eloquently voiced by one of the Sikh women, Neena:

> 'It is strange, is it not, how sometimes a soul will speak to a soul across language, across the generations, across every difference of race and birth and breeding.'

The class were quick to pick up the racial implications. At the beginning of the novel Nicola Gore and the Sikhs regard each other with mutual suspicion; theirs is greater than hers, in view of the madness afflicting English people, and they are reluctant to allow her to accompany them on their flight from London. The class translated this into simple racial rejection. A white girl playing a Sikh in her group's dramatic presentation snapped at the girl playing Nicola, 'We don't want no whites', and a Muslim girl commenting on this section of the book wrote:

> 'Nicky's feelings towards the Sikhs was that she was scared of them and that they were a different colour and they wore different clothes. The Sikhs feelings towards Nicky were that they didn't like her and she was white.'

The message was registered equally speedily, superficially or otherwise it is impossible to tell. In her story a white girl had Nicky say to her parents:

> 'The Sikhs they looked after me and I went with them they are proud people wise and good and allways ready to help in danger they save me and children and make tools and weapons'.

One of the Sikh girls finished off her story in a similar vein, 'I've always hated Indians', said Nicky's Dad, 'But now I think they're the kindest people in the world'. Two girls, one black one white, wrote about their Sikh classmates in their questionnaires:

> 'I know Parmjit and Kulvinder. They are nice and they are my friends. They are very kind they give me sweets and they are not bad. And they cannot eat beef and they have to obey the rules'.

> 'Kulvinder is a Sikh. She's a nice kind of girl. She has adapted to the way we live and has a good personality'.

Kulvinder and Parmjit's own reaction to having their culture so publicly exposed was, understandably enough, guarded defensiveness. A central episode in the novel involves its title. The villagers of Felpham refuse to allow the Sikhs entry, coin myths about their customs and stigmatize them 'the devil's children'. Discussing the episode one group called over Parmjit to advise them on Sikh beliefs; she was decidedly unwilling to help. Meanwhile in her group's discussion, which was taped, Kulvinder was getting adamant, 'Just because they're a different colour doesn't mean they're devil's children'. On the other hand Kulvinder and a Muslim boy expressed approval of the novel's multiracialness in their questionnaires:

'It's not many stories they do mention Sikhs but I'm glad they did'.

'It was set out nicely and did not have only one religion people it was mixed'.

and the Asian children generally had become more open about their cultures by the end of the month. This was particularly noticeable in the session run by the Sikh student teacher when Sikh and Muslim children began to exchange information about language and customs. That the white children learned a lot almost goes without saying. After all at the outset hardly any of them had even been aware that Parmjit and Kulvinder were Sikhs. I recorded only one negative racial comment; that was from a white boy who endorsed the Felpham villagers' distrust of the Sikhs. 'I don't like them', he whispered to me indicating a Muslim boy nearby.

Children who missed sessions through absence or who found it difficult to keep abreast of the story because of problems with reading were at least able to extract some benefit as a result of sharing drama and discussion activities with others who knew exactly what was going on. It was gratifying to have the teaching methodology approved by one white boy who observed in his questionnaire, 'I liked the drama of *The Devil's Children* because it is like being part of the story.' Perhaps the most rewarding experience pedagogically was when a discussion group, on tape, discarded the questions I had set them and initiated their own debate on the novel's merits. The other outcome worth mentioning is that by the end both the evaluator and I thought less well of the novel than when we first read it. The student teacher pointed out that the portrait of the Sikhs exaggerated their virtues and took no account of the cultural adaptations they had made to living in Britain. Positive and generous the portrait may be, but in 1978 it also appears romantic and patronising.

Finally, a caveat about intensive use and evaluation of this kind. As an occasional experiment it can be exciting and instructive, but there are dangers in it becoming the normal classroom approach to reading novels. Fiction, after all, is primarily meant for the pleasure and edification of the individual reader. My heart warmed to the 12 year old boy who said to me, on being issued with the term's class reader, 'Sir, can we just read this without having to discuss it?'

More generally, I hope this chapter has managed to convey a sense of tentativeness and uncertainty, because that is the way I feel about books after two years back in the classroom. Too much of what has been written about them from a multiracial point of view has been strident, overemphatic and humourless. Significantly it has mostly been written by outsiders to the classroom.* Classroom sensitivity is not compatible with that degree of assertiveness. Whatever their importance in our lives we do not really know what books do for us. On what basis, then, can we pretend to be so sure about what they do for others? Deliberately, also, I have said nothing about using books to change children's attitudes. That is not how I feel about books. Nor is it how I feel about my pupils. It is for them to determine what to make of the books they read.

Reference

1   Interested readers will find the full evaluation report in Kathy Stredder's M.Ed thesis (University of Birmingham, 1978). I am indebted to her for giving me access to the data and for noticing so many things I missed in the classroom.

*The only writing by insiders that I know is to be found in *English in Education* Spring 1977 which includes valuable articles by Joan Goody and Hugh Knight.

6 Schools and Racism

'What racialism really boils down to is ... that coloureds used to be inferior to them, when the British were rulers. They just don't want them to be superior.'
15 year old Muslim girl

'If it is a vision of the good life which ultimately determines curriculum content, then this vision cannot be imposed on people. In the long run it must be their own.'
Mary Warnock

Racism* assumes many guises, not least in education. For convenience they can be divided into two categories — institutional and individual. The manifestations of institutional racism include the underperformance of black pupils, all-white curricula, and racist textbooks in school libraries and stock cupboards. Individual racism takes such forms as physical attacks and abuse directed against minority group teachers and pupils, National Front leafleting at school gates, staff prejudices, and hostile white reactions to the introduction of multiracial materials in the classroom. Convenient as the distinction may be, it is important to recognise the broad area of overlap between the two sets of phenomena and, also, the symbiotic nature of the relationship which unites them. Individual racism is both an expression of institutional racism and indispensable to its persistence. A telling illustration was furnished in the summer of 1978 by a report on the underperformance of West Indian children in the London Borough of Redbridge.[1] Undertaken by the local community relations council and a black pressure group, it echoed the findings on underachievement amongst young

*Obviously enough 'racism' in this chapter and elsewhere in the book refers to the white racism endemic in British society. I hope I am not therefore taken to imply that racism is the monopoly of white people. Only historical ignorance, and a cockeyed version of contemporary reality, could support such a view. In finding a footnote necessary I have particularly in mind the anti-white attitudes of a minority of black youngsters which I referred to in the introduction and chapter 1, and which an increasing number of white teachers find so disconcerting. Anti-white attitudes are as much racism as anti-black attitudes, whatever their cause, and they have equally to be combated in school.

blacks recorded by a succession of national and local reports in the early 1970s. They were shown to do less well on standardised tests and in GCE and CSE examinations than their white and Asian peers, and to be overrepresented in ESN schools and remedial units. The report's suggestion that negative stereotypes and expectations on the part of white teachers might be a causative factor was greeted with predictable piety and defensiveness by local representatives of the teachers' unions, whilst the chairman of Redbridge education committee commented, with breathtaking ingenuousness:

> 'In general terms, and I mean this in the nicest possible way, the West Indian children are more interested in the creative activities, in sports.... Do you want a hard-working, high-achieving young man or woman, or do you want to develop their present happy approach and make things up in due course?'

This is an appalling statement — all the more so, given the status of the author, for his obliviousness of the implications of what he is saying. It is also a racist statement, since it rests on the assumption of different educational entitlements for black and white children, and an example of precisely the kind of negative stereotypes about West Indians which the Redbridge report had in mind.

The underachievement of black children in British schools is a complicated phenomenon, and no doubt a complete explication would have to be multifactoral, but there is no gainsaying the fact, attested by the Redbridge and earlier reports, that the negative stereotypes entertained amongst the teaching profession are one potent causative factor. Some commentators have chosen to deduce from this that many white teachers are racists. I do not find such a perspective helpful; indeed it has proved damagingly counterproductive. The chairman of Redbridge education committee intended no racism, no malice towards black children, in saying what he did. I am not exonerating him; obviously he is responsible for his own utterances. But I do not want to call him a racist, nor do I want to call the many teachers who harbour similar stereotypes and prejudices racists. It is more useful to interpret their attitudes as manifestations of institutional racism — legacies of their socialisation into the dominant norms of a racist society. The individual racism represented by demeaning stereotypes is both an expression of the institutional racism deeply embedded in the educational system and a guarantee of its survival. This is what I mean by describing the relationship between the two categories of racism as symbiotic; they are mutually nourishing and interdependent. Having said that, I find it necessary to add, *pace* the teachers' unions, that there is a disconcertingly large minority within the profession which is racist — quite openly and virulently anti-black. I shall return to that minority, and to the whole question of teachers' attitudes, later in the chapter. The bulk of what I want to say pertains to the racism of white pupils and what can be done about it in school.

Two years ago my fourth year CSE group were asked to write to the title 'A modern problem' (taken from a past exam paper) as part of a routine progress test in basic skills — relic of an earlier dispensation and since discarded. Six white pupils elected to write, quite independently of one another, as follows:

'there's a lot of foreiners in this country they have taken a lot of the work, and the pakistanies have a lot of shops here now' (Tony)

'At one time we owned nearly all the world but now we've only got a little piece of the world. There are too many coloureds in our country.' (Sharon)

'Todays problem is that all the imergrants come over and goes onto social security get paid every week and if they have not got no home they put them up in 5 star hotels with all there bills paid by the taxes of the british people ... in our country the imergrants come from pakestain to England so they can have their operation on the natational Ealth because they do not have to pay. The pound is falling because of the imergrants they buy all of the shops and the money they get profits they back to their own country ... there prices are low so more people go to their shops for goods that means the British mans shop go backrupt then the coloureds buy more shops for there brothers' (Simon)

'One of the modern problems in my mind is that there are too many imigrants in England everywhere you look you see Pakistanys and Africans mostly coloured people. I think that they should all go back to their own countries and just leave English people on English soil. The reason why I think we should get them out is because they're taking our houses and shops and if we don't do something about it soon they'll take over our country and then we will be leaving the country ourselves, and another reason is because they come over here and sign on the social security and claim money for themselves and if they are going to

do that they might as well stay over there own country and claim
it there. And another thing when the war was on where was they
then they was all hiding in their mud huts. So I think the government should listen to Enock Powel and get the imigrants out.'
(Dean)

'stop imagration unless the persons can be watched so as they
don't call on *there* friends ... there is not enough done for our on
people in our on country, our goverment provides more for
people abroad than for its own people.' (Barry)

'the problem with today is imigrants! all the pakistanies come
over here and half of them arn't preperd to work so they have
social security, they fill ther house with kids and clame child
benifits they end up better of than if they worked so they send
money over to ther relitives and they come over and it go's on in
one big circul. we sould send them all back home, or stop sociel
security for foreigners.

Pakistanies don't have to ware a crashe helmet on a motor bike
but us get fined if we don't. Even the ones who own shops they
can stay open all night if they want, when the war was on they
went home. If they don't have a house to live in thay put them
up in five star hotels all bills payed.' (George)

To many secondary school teachers this will constitute an all too
familiar array of prejudices, stereotypes and half-truths. They
antedate, of course, the rise of the National Front, although
National Front propaganda may well have contributed to their
presence in these excerpts. With the obvious exception of topical
details such as crash helmets and five star hotels, white pupils of
mine were expressing almost identical opinions fifteen years ago,
and I particularly recall the unabashed glee with which the advent
of Alf Garnett to the television screen was greeted. There are two
other points to underscore. First, such opinions are not suddenly
formed at fourteen; they have been in the making, as chapter one
attempted to show, since their exponents were in nursery school:
and, secondly, none of the latter were ogres of racial hatred. I liked
and got on reasonably well, bar the odd classroom skirmish, with
them all. Their writing puts me in mind of a striking passage in
Jeremy Seabrook's book on Blackburn, *City Close-Up*. After quot-
ing at length from a group of elderly white working-class women,
bemoaning the iniquities of the 'Pakis', he comments:

'What is taking place is only secondarily an expression of

prejudice. It is first and foremost a therapeutic psychodrama, in which the emotional release of its protagonists takes precedence over what is actually being said. They inveigh against the immigrants much as they might inveigh against poverty, privation and old age. It is an expression of their pain and powerlessness confronted by the decay and dereliction, not only of the familiar environment, but of their own lives, too — an expression for which our society provides no outlet. Certainly it is something more complex and deep-rooted than what the metropolitan liberal evasively and easily dismisses as prejudice.' (Penguin edition, 1973.)

Patently my fourteen year olds had not suffered in quite this way, but they were also victims, in a sense, of processes and forces which, to judge by their writing, they had hardly begun to comprehend. They too found a ready scapegoat for their ills in racial minorities, and it would be equally facile to dismiss what they had to say on race as simply prejudice. What, then, is to be made of it, and, above all, what is to be done about it?

A portrait of Barry (quote five above) can serve to provide the beginning of an answer. He was of National Front parentage and himself sympathetic to the party's racist views. At school he was an awkward customer, a classic case of the authoritarian personality, alternating between obsequiousness and truculence, and incapable of revising his views in the face of fresh evidence. On one occasion, during the course of a language unit, he steadfastly refused to accept that only 11% of the world's population speak English as a mother tongue ('What about all the whites in Rhodesia?') and that more speak Chinese and Hindi. Possessed of a keen sense of his rights and utter contempt for the 'establishment', because it threatened those rights, he found inspiration and solace, like many of his white peers, in the anarchic lyrics of punk rock and the conspiracy theory of the National Front according to which there is a plot afoot to deprive the Englishman of his right to speak his mind. 'At 16,' he wrote in an essay, 'I am all mixed up. I am against what I am moulded out to be by society. I am kicking against the system.' His concern for individual rights and liberties was genuine enough. His list of infringements did not stop short at race relations legislation; indeed it included some surprises. The decision of the Schools Council programme committee early in 1978 not to publish the multiracial education project's report in its original form was covered in the local evening paper together with my comments.

Many of my pupils read the column and were merely puzzled as to what it was all about. Barry fully understood the issues at stake; he was incensed that anyone should have the gall (let alone the power) to deny publication to a report on the ground that they did not like what it said.

On race his behaviour was a good deal more accommodating than his public pronouncements might have led one to suppose. I have already referred in chapter one to the many cases of white children who sense no incongruity in being repatriationists and having black friends. Barry was such a case. He got on remarkably well with black and Asian pupils, many of whom had been his classmates since infant school. Once he confided to me his special admiration for Delroy, a black contemporary, who had as many white friends as black and enjoyed punk rock as much as reggae and had, therefore, to run the gauntlet of gibes such as 'pork-lover' from other black pupils. Underneath Barry's prickly obduracy there was a more general sensitivity which manifested itself particularly in his response to literature. During the CSE course *Animal Farm*, the poetry of Wilfred Owen and Siegfried Sassoon and the Australian novel *Walkabout* were three pieces of literature which struck strong intellectual and emotional chords for him. Reading the first World War poetry inspired him to write passionate verse of his own; *Animal Farm* took him to the local library to borrow books on Marx and Lenin; and Nicholas Roeg's film of *Walkabout*, which adds to the book's themes some compelling sequences on the white man's exploitation of the aborigine, prompted the following:

> 'the scenes of beauty and the cruelty of how the white man is exploiting the aborigines in their own land made a very fascinating film ... it also showed how the two cultures can converse even without a matching language, and so primitive people are not so dumb as people make out.'

It is only fair to add that Barry found in the Australian situation confirmation for his repatriationism — the Aborigine's right to Australia being comparable, in his view, to the right of the indigenous white man to Britain.

Eventually, in his fifth year, Barry became head boy. At the school head boy and girl were chosen by an electorate comprising staff and pupils. The event had all the trappings of general and local elections — ballot boxes, voting slips, and so forth — and it was undoubtedly a valuable experience, for staff and pupils alike, of political democracy. However, even though Barry was voted in by a massive majority, several members of staff queried the wisdom of a system that could elevate to a position of prestige and influence a pupil notorious for his National Front sympathies. I understood and respected their concern, but believed it to be unwarranted; indeed I voted for Barry myself, because I thought he would make an excellent head boy, and it did not prove necessary for me or anyone else to urge the head of upper school, who also championed his cause, to take him on one side and underline the precise nature of his office's obligations in a multiracial school — advice he accepted in the best possible way. As things turned out, Barry was not a good head boy, nor was his final year at school a particularly distinguished one. But on the question of race he was diplomacy itself.

I feel confident about this portrait of Barry in a way that I do not about the portrait of the black girl Phyllis in chapter one (even if divided by social class, we were united by race), and I want to extract two general points from it. One has to do with analysis, the other with action. First, the portrait demonstrates the complexity of racial attitudes (that there is, for instance, no easy relationship between attitudes and behaviour) and how one pupil's racism is inextricably (or so it seems) bound up with a whole lot of other puzzling and paradoxical personality traits. Secondly, the school's successful accommodation of a racist head boy makes a statement about how schools should properly proceed on race in a democracy; namely, that those of us who work in multiracial schools and believe in democracy are going to have to learn to live as best we can with the kind of white racism exemplified by Barry and his peers.

The concept of democracy is at the heart of the parallel debate over what to do about the National Front. I should like to turn to that debate for a moment because it clarifies some classroom issues. There are many who argue that, since the Front is an unmitigated evil, it should be 'smashed'; which may include any or all of — denying it access to public platforms and the media; disrupting its meetings and the distribution of its literature; stopping its meetings and the distribution of its literature; stopping its marches; and proscribing it. Certainly I take the Front to be an evil organisation, but I have no wish to 'smash' it. On the contrary I defend its rights as a legal political party in a parliamentary democracy, even its right to hold public meetings in multiracial schools at election time.* The curtailment of those rights not only 'impairs democracy

*In the bicentenary of his death it is perhaps appropriate to recall the remark attributed to Voltaire: "I disapprove of what you say, but I will defend to the death your right to say it."

itself', to borrow a phrase from a *New Statesman* editorial (August 19th, 1977), but also inadvertently furthers the Front's cause by fuelling the conspiracy theory to which I have already referred. Similarly, I maintain, it would have been ideologically and strategically disastrous had the authorities at Barry's school decided to suspend its democratic traditions on account of his known racist views.*

In the past year considerable publicity has surrounded a National Front campaign to introduce its literature into schools. Once again there have been 'smashers' of racism who have insisted that teachers should either physically stop the distribution of Front leaflets at school gates or at least confiscate them from pupils after they have been distributed. One headteacher has said he would call the police, on the ground that leaflet distribution posed a threat to peace and order, and one LEA — significantly (dare I suggest?) one with a poor record on multiracial education — has said it will suspend pupils found distributing Front literature. Frankly I find these reactions, putative or otherwise, absurd and almost calculated to drive already alienated white youngsters into Front membership. Whether teachers like it or not, the school has to find a forum of some kind within its walls for the discussion of the Front's ideas and literature once they make their presence felt. I would not want to pretend that the task will be an easy one. In schools with poor race relationships it may prove well nigh impossible. But the attempt has to be made, for the school is probably the only place in most children's experience where it can be undertaken with a semblance of rationality. As a sample of what can be achieved I offer what Marcia, a third year black girl, wrote after reading a National Front leaflet in the classroom:

Racial Hatred

'You may have heard about Enoch Powell wanting repatriation recently in Britain. My view is that if Enoch Powell got every black person in the United Kingdom out, then this country would be lost. I think that basically Blacks are the main working force of Britain. A recent survey showed that West Indians and East Indians tend to do more work than the British. Why didn't Enoch Powell open his big mouth when the Blacks first came over here?

---

* Sadly, this is just what they did do in the following year, when voting rights were restricted to members of staff.

Why was he so quiet when Britain needed Blacks to build up this country? He must think we're like disposable plastic cups. Use them then throw them away.

Most innocent West Indians came to this country because they were promised a new and better life. They came. They worked for long hours every day to earn their bread, help build up the country and now when they're just ready to reap the benefits Mr Powell wants them thrown out.

I think racial hatred is stemmed from the early days when slavery was abolished. I don't think the majority of the whites could bring theirselves to accept the Black Man as an equal. Because for so long he has been looked down upon. It's true Blacks were naive of the Whites ways and perhaps lacked in areas of intelligence. Resulting in the Whites taking advantage of the Blacks. And believe me, the Blacks really suffered. After a 150 years the Black man was finally made free. I think people believe that we should have been kept in slavery, where we could have been safely kept down. When you look at it in general really it all seems so idiotic all because my skin is darker than yours.

One thing I am pleased about though, is that the younger generation of Whites are not prejudiced — unlike their elders. You can see this even in school.

Another big issue today in Britain's main cities is *violence* especially among Black youths.

If you expect me to jump quickly to their defence and say — oh how they can't help it and that it's the pressures of today's society, then you're in for a suprise, because I'm not. Of course society has to share the blame but muggings are inexcusable.

I think for anyone who really wants to understand the Black man they should read one of his newspapers, not the sort of anti-white ones they have about now, but a good paper like the 'West Indian World' honestly some stories I read in that paper would really make you cry. All his life the Black Man has been intimidated and looked down upon. All his life he has had to settle for second best. And I think now that today's West Indians are realising that fact and want to do something about it.

That's why many black people today hate the white man generally. Although its a narrow minded view of life it just simply represents their feelings. Perhaps the majority of Blacks are being ignorant about things, but Racial Hatred is a big, bad fact, and I've got a feeling something big and bad is going to happen —

there's going to be a big explosion *Soon*!!
    If I have offended anyone — black or white — with this piece of
writing I'd like to assure you it was done unintentionally'.[2]

To revert to the writing of the white fourteen year olds with which I
began, I want now to suggest that curtailing the National Front's
legitimate entitlements is of the same order as trying to gag white
racism in the classroom — ideologically and strategically dangerous
— and that young white racists have as much right as anyone else to
expect to find attentive adult ears at school. There are teachers who
maintain that the media's problematic approach to race (invited,
perhaps, by the essay title 'A modern problem' my fourth years were
addressing themselves to) should find no echo in the school
curriculum — on the basis of the completely untested claim that
racist views will be confirmed by dint of being given an airing in the
respectable ethos of the classroom. Admittedly the evaluation of the
work of Lawrence Stenhouse and his colleagues in the field of
teaching about race relations does show that classroom relationships can founder, even disintegrate, as a result. But race, after all,
is an issue, whether we like it or not, and, although I do not conduct
class discussions on race relations, in the way that I did fifteen years
ago, I have attempted to multiracialise the English curriculum,
which may well, as the two previous chapters have shown, yield
similar effects.
    Some teachers think it appropriate to try to exclude the sort of
remarks I quoted in chapters four and five ('This is an imposition
on white people', 'I don't want to read about coloureds' etc.) with
rebukes of the 'Not in my classroom, thank you very much' ilk.
Understandably these are resented by white pupils who see in them
confirmation of the National Front's conspiracy theory. I do not
mean it is never appropriate to invoke the school's disciplinary
authority. Teachers who stood by idly in the face of racial bullying,
racial taunting or racial vandalism would obviously be guilty of
professional irresponsibility. But comments like 'This is an imposition on white people' do not fall into any of these categories. They
are made, more often than not, by vulnerable white children —
dispossessed, or so they feel, of their corner shops, their cinemas,
their housing and job prospects, and now confronted with the
possibility of losing the school curriculum too. Frequently such
children are guilty of personal racial abuse as well. Once when I was
on dinner duty a hefty black fourth year boy reported to me that a
third year white boy had called him a 'wog' following a squabble

over a water jug. The culprit was one of the most pathetic chldren I have ever taught — stunted, unattractive and of very low ability, regularly himself the target of taunts (directed at the fact that he was dirty, bedraggled and smelled) which every now and then unleashed in him uncontrollable paroxysms of temper and violence. The black boy had a reputation for trying to solve problems with his fists; in reporting the incident to me, rather than thumping the culprit, he tacitly recognized, I felt, that the latter was a victim too.

White racist children, for the most part, need support and sympathy, not gagging — support best extended, in my experience, through small group discussion led by a concerned but uncensorious teacher. This is an unthreatening context for the exchange of views which, I believe, can serve a genuinely therapeutic function in allowing children to explore freely their deepest anxieties about race. Barry was one pupil who very much welcomed the opportunity provided by discussion of this kind. I hope I am not taken to imply that it is only a matter of letting white racists have their heads. Their myths and prejudices have certainly to be challenged — but challenged in a way which strikes them ultimately as supportive. The wrong kind of challenge is represented by the widely recommended but intimidating exercises in critical appreciation of the media (saying, in effect, 'Now let's just look at this *Sun* nonsense about five star hotels') which end up by being simply alienating. If the challenge comes from other white children it is best of all. Peter, a white fourth year, came into my room before school one Monday morning and picked up the issue of *New Internationalist* I had brought in with me. It was devoted to the question of race. 'You're always bringing in stuff about coloureds,' he said and proceeded to tell me about his weekend in all-white St. Asaph with his grandmother. 'I didn't see a single coloured in St. Asaph. When a black group came on "Top of the Pops", my nan said, "Get those wogs off."' After a pause he added, as though to leave me in no doubt, 'I can't stand coloureds.' Mandy, a white girl in Peter's class with whom I had been talking when he came in, saved me the trouble of fumbling for a suitable reply. Not normally one to engage in that kind of debate, and in any case no lover of 'Pakis' (by her own admission on another occasion), she surprised me by taking Peter to task. 'What', she said sharply, 'You mean you don't like Sandra?' Sandra was a black friend of hers whom Peter enjoyed a gibing but strong relationship with. Visibly taken aback he said sheepishly, 'Well, she's all right, I suppose.'

The most effective form of challenge by teachers is a concerted attack on institutional racism — that is, the development of unambiguously multiracial policies for curriculum and organisation, even if in the short term they actually generate more manifestations of individual racism. Some of the details in the writing by Barry and his friends (e.g. 'when the war was on where was they then they was all hiding in their mud huts') would suggest that their school at least had a fairly long road to travel before reaching that goal. Pupils, also, will want to know where their teachers stand on race; if the relationship between teacher and pupils is sufficiently open, occasions for meeting this perfectly legitimate expectation will arise in the classroom readily and naturally. For instance in January 1978 the Asian pupils in my fifth year tutor group commented disapprovingly on the uncalled for observations of Judge McKinnon following the acquittal of Kingsley Read, a former National Front stalwart, on an incitement to racial hatred charge. Shortly afterwards they were further angered by Mrs. Thatcher's call for a 'clear end of immigration' on the basis of white people's fear that 'fundamental British characteristics which have done so much for the world' would be 'rather swamped by people of a different culture' (*The Observer* 5th February 1978). 'She shouldn't have said that, sir,' said Rashida coming into class next morning, 'She shouldn't do that, should she?' 'No,' I agreed, and I explained that the remark looked to me like calculated vote-catching.

On the other hand there are obviously dangers in striking one's pupils as, in their word, 'unfair' over race. Shortly after my arrival at the school one of Barry's friends asked me in class *à propos* of nothing in particular, 'What do you think of the National Front, sir?' 'Oh,' I said unguardedly, 'A bit sick in the head mostly.' Whilst this rejoinder earned me the plaudits of Rashida sitting nearby — 'Yeah, that's true, that is,' — it hardly endeared me to the questioner or to Barry whose parents I had unwittingly consigned to mental hospital. Much has been written about the bad relationships existing between white teachers and black pupils and about the negative stereotypes (such as those the Redbridge report highlighted) the former hold of the latter. Nothing, so far as I know, has been written about the minority of white teachers who are more than half in love with their black pupils (their panache, their humour, their charm), nor about how this is bitterly resented by just those white pupils who are least able to tolerate rivalry for the teacher's affection and attention. 'Let's face it, sir,' said Jane, a white fourth year, during a comparatively minor contretemps, 'There's only one thing wrong with me as far as you're concerned. I haven't got a coloured skin.' What left me speechless was partly the venom with which this was uttered and partly how I had ever managed to convey to even one embittered child such an impression. Some years ago at another school a white pupil complained to me that 'Mrs X' only ever took 'wogs' in her car for out of school trips and activities. I had not noticed it at the time, but subsequent observation showed the complaint to be well-founded. It is important, of course, not to confuse racial favouritism with taking a firm and forthright stand on racism.

I have said that in my experience the best forum for exploring the issue of race is small group discussion led by a concerned but uncensorious teacher. It has also been my experience that the most successful kind of input, whether to stimulate talking or writing, is literature or film in which the voice is unmistakeably that of other children inviting comparisons with their experience and assessment of their viewpoint. Where the voice is adult (television presenter, novelist, teacher), and an adult voice moreover purporting to give children the 'real facts' and telling them, in effect, what they should be thinking, it is highly likely (and quite rightly) to be ignored and rejected. Two television programmes, for instance, in the BBC series *Scene*, in both of which the voice was young and authentic, prompted almost wholly sympathetic responses and led to lively discussion and writing. The first was the 'access' programme made by a group of Brixton girls on the subject of being young, black and British. I used it with third, fourth and fifth year groups and after time for discussion suggested they write down their reactions in the form of letters to the black girls. Here are a sample of extracts:

'I liked your film very much. I agree with you it is very hard for black people in this country. Black people find it very hard to get a job, because I know someone who has been trying to get a job since he left school, and he is black. And it is true what people say if a white girl goes out with a black boy they call her a "wog lover" and your family say you are a disgrace to the family, the same goes for the black family. I sympathize with you a lot.'
Third year white girl

'I enjoyed your programme very much and I think it is right that people no matter what colour they are should all be treated the same. I liked the part where the people are having a festival. Although there was a lot of coloured people there, there was also a few white people. It would be better if people got to know each

other better, then perhaps more white people, would join coloured people's entertainment and coloured people would join in whites too. I hope your programme has proved to some people that we're all the same whatever the colour.'
Fourth year mixed race girl

'I know how you feel. You should have the same rights as everyone else. But there is one thing you can't complain about. All Pakistanis and Jamaicans getting the old houses. Because where I live there are new houses everywhere around. And there are Pakistanis and Jamaicans in nearly every row. And there are homeless white people as well as them.'
Fourth year white girl

'I understand your problem about blacks and whites. But you must also understand that white people have a lot of problems too like getting jobs. Also you say that people call you names, but blacks also call whites names. In the secondary school I go to all colours seem to get on well together even though we do seem to group sometimes. I hope you see my point as well as I see yours.'
Thrid year white girl

'Your programme was not very good on the hardships of black people. It lacked interviews. Therefore we do not know what the black people think about it. If you're going to show black culture show it with a little more rhythm and music and a little more style. Try talking to the actual people in the ghetto and you would have a good programme.'
Third year black boy

'I see your point of view about being black and being offended when someone calls you a wog but white people get offended when they are called white honkeys. Also it is not just black people who doesn't get jobs when they go for an interview because you also see a lot of white people at the Labour Exchange. I don't think nothing can stop black people going round with other black people neither the same with white people. But you proved your point.'
Third year mixed race girl

'Dear Jungle Bunnies,
   I liked your programme because you told the truth, not like

some TV programmes where they live in a fantasy world.
Yours,
   John'
Fourth year white boy

'I think white people think of you as second class people. They
don't give you fair chances in life. I am not white myself but
European and they fear much about us. I hope somebody comes
up with an organisation for coloured people in England.'
Third year Greek Cypriot boy

'I was extremely annoyed about your programme about racialism, mainly because you seem to think that you were being picked
on or neglected because of white people causing trouble, but
don't you agree that there are a lot of black people looking for
trouble? For example, read a newspaper and see who the people
are; mainly you will read, a boy was mugged near Handsworth
today we believe the culprit was a West Indian boy. But don't
get me wrong. I am not prejudiced but I would like to get a point
clear. A lot of coloureds are nice sociable people but there are
some really rough ones who claim to be Rastas and they always
cause trouble. Anyway I hope your feelings against white people
become more friendly and I would like to see more black and
white people get together and make life have more freedom for
everyone.'
Fifth year white boy

'I'd like to congratulate you for your film about racial discrimination. I can sympathise with you as I myself am an Asian girl, but I
am glad to say that many of my problems concerning racial
prejudice are now erased. I think the programme was very well
presented especially to show how little children don't seem to
notice the differences between them in colour. If there were no
other influences from elsewhere like from parents or other adults,
the children as they grew up would not question the differences of
coloured people because they had accepted them.
   At school, like you showed in the programme, I think we widen
our scope when we get to know other children and we might find
that we can be really good friends. I think the people who are
colour prejudiced are usually the ones who are unsure of their
information. Sometimes I know the parents have a lot to do with
it and also what they have heard as gossip or passing remarks to
suggest unpleasant things about coloured people.

As you pointed out where racial discrimination really exists is with jobs. Some people in Britain are quite sure that unemployment is due to the large amount of coloured people in this country. I definitely don't believe that and think sometimes that it is an injustice when coloured people are refused jobs even though they have the qualifications. Some people have a right to jobs in Britain you pointed this out by using the pictures of the last group of coloured people as they came to this country.

Although you showed the buildings in which the coloured people were living in a bad state, I have to disagree with you, because I do not think the living conditions are quite that bad. Of course I may not be right and I certainly have not seen all the places where coloured people live, but I do know that around here they all have quite good houses and homes. Even at school I think most people are on friendly terms but it might be because it is only a small school, or, I think that it is mostly because instead of staying aloof and apart from other races we have begun to understand each other's manner and behaviour, culture and religion and I know that this has a lot to do with it. I do believe and agree with you that we can live together, of course I can say that for school, but for myself I don't think I can socially, as strict religious customs hold me back and others of my religion, but then that is another subject.'
Fifth year Muslim girl

I have quoted the final letter in its entirety both because it is a remarkable piece of writing and also because it represents a level of sweet reasonableness, achieved without making any concessions to racism, which one wishes all children, and adults, could aspire to. The overwhelming majority of my pupils, whichever year they were in, accepted, albeit (in the case of white children) often grudgingly or with reservations, that black people have a raw deal in British society and that we can and should (this was the programme's concluding emphatic point) learn to live together. There were, of course, predictably discordant white reactions, as there were to the other television programme 'Welcome to Britain', in which a teenage Ugandan Asian boy, whose family were expelled by President Amin's edict in 1972, described his family's first weeks adjusting to a new life in Scotland. Again most of my pupils responded warmly and sympathetically, admiring the hospitality of the Scots and appreciating the signs of interracial friendship and intercultural understanding highlighted by the film. But two white third year girls chose to write as follows:

> 'I think that they should send some of them back to Uganda, because there are too many of them around here. They should go somewhere else if they have got expelled from Uganda. There is an awful lot in Birmingham, far too many actually. They come over bringing some diseases with them and give them to everyone else. A lot of them have scabies and some come to school's and give scabies to us.*'

> 'I think that the Asians are a smelly lot. They are very rude, especially the older ones. They seem to have got one English custom, picking up young white girls who are daft enough to go with them. They make out that they are all very goody goody but in actual fact they are sneaky and underhand. They seem to get on very well. This could be because they stick together and help each other out. This would make them very unpopular and pro-bably explains why they are persecuted.'

The most effective book for engaging teenagers with the issue of racism I have found to be Farrukh Dhondy's excellent collection of stories *East End at Your Feet* (Macmillan Topliner). These six stories about white and Asian youngsters growing up in the East End of London are told with verve and humour from the youngster's own point of view. Several focus on the predicament of Asian boys and girls caught between two cultures. One or two confront the experience of racism forthrightly and vividly. The most poignant is 'KBW' which describes through the eyes of a white boy a racist attack on the Bengali family who are his neighbours. I used the story with my fifth year group as part of their CSE course work; asking them to write an essay comparing the story's presentation of racism with their own experience. Many wrote strongly and movingly. I reproduce below extracts from the writing of (in order) a white girl, a Muslim girl, a Hindu girl and a Sikh boy:

> 'The same thing happened with a family of Bangalis who moved into our road. The neighbours didn't like black people so they started to talk about them telling each other that they had seen horrible things happening in the Bangalis home. This started the children calling them names and hitting them. One woman threw a brick through their window but nobody got hurt, but the

---

*A recent scabies outbreak at the school had started with a Pakistani family.

Bangali family had had enough of it so they moved somewhere else.'*

'Although I personally haven't sufferred any racialist attacks, I think my dad has had enough experience of prejeudice against coloureds. When I first came to Britain I didn't expect anything like colour prejeudice. I had thought that the British were far too sensible. So at school at first there was the usual jokes and jearing, but I thought it was just the children who liked to make fun, so I was very surprised to hear that even Adults had the same prejeudice. I wouldn't believe it at first that many of the good office clerical vacanies had all been refused to my dad without any good reason what so ever. But, the reason most of them seemed to give was that they simply couldn't believe the references he had. The references were very good and praised my dad in clerk accountancy. So, the job that my dad had done since he left school was turned down by all the offices, because they didn't want a coloured working with them. My dad looked for a job for a long time and was constantly refused, so he decided that he would change from an office worker to hard labour in factories. I felt that this reduced him somehow in grade. The memory of these first few months still make me feel bitter against the employers who could be so irrational, and I know my dad feels the same way. Sometimes he would even try to be proud about it, because he says that his references were so good that they couldn't believe it, but I know he is really being sarcastic. To me it just hurts to think that my dad wasn't given a chance, even a little one at any good job. Since then my dad has done various jobs including courses in Government Training Centres so it isn't intelligence that he lacks. But, now he just does a small job although it does need brains, and it doesn't pay a lot. I think that it is injustice for at finding jobs my dad seems to be unlucky. I just cannot understand why people can be so irrational about

* I later discovered that the family of the reserved white girl who was the author of this had themselves suffered racist harassment. Originally they lived in a town on the edge of the West Midlands conurbation. Following the break up of her marriage the mother took a Pakistani lover. This led to her being abused and on one occasion physically assaulted in the street. For their own safety they moved to the multiracial community surrounding the school and the mother began to adopt elements of her lover's culture — observing Ramadhan, piercing her nostril with a jewel and cooking and eating curry in Asian style.

racialism and colour when people all over the world have the same feelings, mind and heart. It is ridiculous to think that just because somebody's skin is a different colour then they assume that the person is dumb. Perhaps people like the National Front should give a really good reason for their opposition against coloureds because so far I haven't heard any yet.

'I think that now racialism is getting better and more fair because of the new act of racial discrimination. But, personally I think what racialism really boils down to is not of the colour, but language or their origin and that coloureds used to be inferior to them, when the British were rulers. They just don't want them to become superior.'

'Myself, I haven't had many or any experiences towards racialism yet. Only the odd one or two. But my sister has had an experience which would have changed her whole life. She worked in a supermarket, one of the popular ones, but the branch she worked at, the market was smaller. There weren't any other ashians around, but there was one, but she left because of racialist remarks. The first few weeks went very nicely and she liked it a lot. Then it happened. It was on a Friday night. She usually worked late on Fridays' because of late customers. But this Friday she was very late. The thing was that she was accused of stealing three pounds. They suspected her because it was her till. Because at the end of the day, they are supposed to take their tills to the manager's office, where the money is to be counted. That's when they told her that three pounds were missing from her till. She didn't know she was the one they suspected, until the manager told her that he was calling the police and that if she wanted to say anything, she'd have to wait until the police arrived. She was all confused and didn't know what to say or do. The police came and there was a police man and a police woman. They started questioning her and trying to make her surrender because she had said that she didn't take the money. Then the police took her to a local station for a statement. But when they got there, they told her she wouldn't be able to go home until she pleaded guilty and that they could put her in a jail and keep her in it until she pleads guilty. And if she did plead guilty they wouldn't make a big thing out of it. So she had to agree because she didn't have a choice. That was the end of it all. She left the job. But from that day on she kept on being miserable and crying and it was the same with my mum. Then she took a course in college and in that college she had to write an essay on some sort of subject and it was on knowledge or experience. So she wrote about her experience with the Supermarket. But she didn't write it as if it had happened to her, but just out of knowledge. Anyhow this teacher read it and asked her about it. And my sister told her every thing and how they'd cheated her into pleading guilty. The teacher asked my sister if she had thought of making a case against the police and the supermarket. My sister said she had and she knew she couldn't win, with all the people against her and especially the police. But the teacher said that she could try and that it wouldn't do any harm. So she did try. The teacher also gave my sister a name of an ashian solicitor. It took at least a year to finish the case. All through the case she had been very tough and she was still thinking that she couldn't win. There was my mum praying at home and saying that it depended on God what happens. But my sister didn't take that in knowledge because, already so much had happened to her. And when she heard that she was found not guilty, she began to cry, she could hardly believe it. Even the judge made a remark that, saying that she had been brave all through the case but when she won it she started crying.

I realized then that there is racialism everywhere even in the police force. But we don't know if the case was out of racialism or something else.

And to think if it wasn't for the teacher, who was white herself, my sister's life would have still been miserable.'

'I think its a very true picture of racialism comparing to my knowledge and experience, I heard on TV that an Indian boy was murdered by the national Front and a couple of days later the Indians stopped a car in the middle of the road on which there wasn't much traffic and smashed all the windows on it and beat the driver to hell because he was a white. I myself almost got in trouble when I walked between the blacks and the whites after there had been Political voting near Soho Road. It was at 9.30 pm I went to Soho Rd to the cinema and as I was walking along Soho Rd I noticed something different about it, there were crowds of people on each side and they all seemed to be black, but the blacks were on one side and the whites on the other. There were more blacks then the whites. The blacks were shouting to the whites and swearing to them. The pavements were packed with people. They were so over crowded that I couldn't find a place to get on the pavement so I walked on the road, as I walked further and further towards the cinema, the population seemed to grow. At last I finally got to the cinema but I couldn't find a place to sneak in through the crowd, there wastn't even a little space you could see through, it was crowded like ants on sugar or bees on a honey comb. In front of the cinema there were all white people and I had to go through them to get in the cinema. Opposite the cinema on the other pavement were the blacks, as I was trying to get through the whites to get in, some one from the back called "hey maan what ya doing there come here." It sounded like a big voice. I looked back it was like a zoo, the blacks had now started to throw stones and bricks. None of them got me because I was half way through by the time the police had arrived to take the beating of stones and bricks but they had shields in front and I was in the cinema safely.'*

On the other hand the most gifted pupil in the group, a white boy, declined to do any writing although he had seemed interested in the story. 'You see, sir,' he said, 'I am a racialist. What I wrote would be racialist. The examiner will mark me down.' I assured him that this would not happen and pointed out that, although his course work folder would be externally moderated, its marking was primarily my responsibility. But there was no persuading him; the conspiracy theory had sunk deep roots.

The case for giving young white racists a voice in school is not based entirely on tactical considerations — providing a safety valve — important as they are. It is a matter of principle, of rights, too. Perhaps I can make my essential point most conclusively in the following way. One of my aims is to develop an 'open' classroom — 'open' in its patterns of communication; and 'open' in the relationship between teacher and learners. Given that aim, I could not possibly justify, even if I wanted to, adding the qualification that actually it is 'closed' to all those thoughts, feelings and experiences children have which I do not want to hear about. My pupils quickly learn that their racial and cultural identities, encounters and aspirations are welcome in classroom talk and writing. These extracts convey some idea of the variety of response I get:

'One day me and my mum went to town and as we were waiting for the bus this lady walked up and just stood in front of us. Well anyway I said, "Do you mind?" and she said, "What did you say?"

*The events described here took place after a National Front meeting during the by-election campaign in Ladywood, Birmingham, in August 1977.

And I said, "Do you mind?" And she said, "I belong to this
country so just get lost where you came from." (She was white)'
Third year Sikh girl as part of work on friends and enemies

'There were very few white people and very few Pakistanis and a
lot of Jamaicans. They were big and tall and I was afraid of
them. They were fighting all the time.'
Fifth year Pakistani boy recalling early days at school

'I went skating the other week and on the way out I was with a few
friends and just happened to look up. Approaching me were 10
Rastafarians. I looked at them and turned away. They then
chased me down the skating ramp and up the road. They almost
caught me. I was lucky, but what about the kids who are not so
lucky?'
Fourth year white boy as part of work on groups and gangs

All are authentic pieces of writing. It would be inconceivable to
disqualify any because one does not want them to be true or because
putting the experience down on paper might make things worse or
for whatever reason. Either the classroom is 'open' in the sense I
have defined or it is 'closed'.

It is at this point (somewhere very near it at least) that I find
myself at odds with the only book about teaching in the multiracial
classroom worth reading — Chris Searle's compilation of children's
writing *The World in a Classroom* (Writers and Readers Publishing
Cooperative). It is an inspiring book, full of splendid writing by
second and third year East Enders, testimony to strikingly imagina-
tive and committed team teaching. The conviction behind the
development of the course was that the classroom, particularly the
English classroom, has an important part to play in the fight
against racism. Its content incorporates the local and the international, in the mutually reinforcing way advocated in chapter 2,
drawing widely on topical events in the East End and its 'anti-fascist
history' and the experience of oppression in Africa, America and
Southern Europe. There are two emphases in the presentation of
the course and in the children's writing which I would endorse —
first, our common humanity and the unmistakeable possibilities
held out by the multiracial classroom for living together harmon-
iously ('Our class can prove to all prejudiced people all over the
world that people from different nations can live together.'); and,
secondly, the curriculum riches the multiracial classroom offers

to teachers who are prepared to take advantage of them.

Where I part company from Searle and his colleagues is in those aspects of their work which seem to me to constitute a pretty clear-cut case of indoctrination. An almost, but not quite, stated objective of the course could be said to be that all children should become socialists and see themselves (and their teachers) as 'undeniably' members of the British working class. Near the beginning of the book Searle writes that the classroom is 'a vital powerhouse' for the teacher committed to the socialist transformation of society and the fight against racism, and towards its end concludes that one of the course's successes was 'our gathering knowledge of belonging to the continuing struggle of working people of the past and present all over the world, for a more just and loving world.' Counting myself neither a socialist nor a member of the working-class (apart from in the obvious sense that I am an employee), I find this hard to take. Moreover, it is just the kind of imposition children need to be protected from. Teachers have no business thrusting their cherished ideologies on young and malleable minds; it is for children to determine for themselves where they stand politically and culturally. They are not going to be helped in the realisation of this inalienable right by the kind of biased version of 'oppression' offered by Searle and his colleagues. Their version confines the phenomenon, by and large, to right-wing dictatorships and white colonialism; left-wing dictatorship and black tyrants find little place. My other reservation about the book is that it gives an unsatisfactory account of racism in school. We are told that it must be challenged consistently — 'exposed, taken on and dealt with' — but are shown little evidence of this taking place. I miss a substantial representation of the white racist voice and, more generally, any sense of the cut and thrust of classroom reality.

Finally I should like to revert to the racism of white teachers. There is a sense, of course, in which we are all racists — the sense (mentioned at the beginning of the chapter) that we have all been socialized into the dominant norms of a racist society. The racism which concerns me here, however, is teacher behaviour which, directly or indirectly, incontrovertibly threatens or impedes the self-realization of black children. I distinguish two forms of such behaviour — behaviour which is motivated by malice towards minority pupils and behaviour which may have similar effects but is the reflection of something else. As I have already claimed, no one with any experience of working in multiracial schools (or all-white ones, for that matter) could possibly deny that there is a small minority in the profession which is virulently anti-black (whether they are Powellites or National Front members or whatever is neither here nor there). Its existence can be illustrated by an experience of mine some six years ago. I was teaching a small withdrawal group of West Indian children in a secondary school one morning. The room I used had a glass door, which meant that anyone passing had a clear view of whoever was inside. On this occasion a senior member of staff passed, paused and looked in. He opened the door, grinned at me and said in a voice loud enough for all to hear, 'Excuse me, is this Dudley Zoo?' When first discussing this incident in print[3] I argued that the teacher concerned was guilty of professional incompetence and professional misconduct and should have been sacked, as should any other whose presence in a school was demonstrably to the detriment of minority race children. Shortly afterwards I received a letter from a former colleague who recalled the incident and correctly identified the teacher. In his letter he wrote: ' ... X is a very complex character who seems to spend the whole of his life throwing off his working class antecedents and becoming more middle class than the middle class themselves. This has led to a quite ostentatious racism which he does not follow through in practice. Although he is capable of making the inane and insensitive remark you quote, he has to my knowledge always been extremely kind and non-racist in his general close contacts with coloured children. I was always rather surprised to learn from the coloured kids at school that he was not the real object of their dislike and that there were others far higher up the list.' I take this as an important corrective which somewhat reinforces what I have already said about the complexity of racial attitudes.

There is a far greater number of teachers who, often with the best will in the world, manage to get themselves in a tangle with black pupils through ignorance, thoughtlessness or sheer insensitivity. Whilst at a different secondary school in the West Midlands to the one in the first anecdote, I was a member of a small group of staff and pupils who went on a hostelling weekend in Wales. When we arrived at the hostel on the Friday night, the teacher in charge asked the children to have their YHA cards ready for handing in to the warden. 'Got your passport, Millicent?' quipped another teacher to a British-born black third year girl (one of that category of black children frequently and mindlessly dismissed by white teachers as having 'chips on their shoulders'). Millicent glowered at him. 'Sorry,' he said realizing his jest had misfired. 'You don't seem to think that's funny.' 'No, I don't,' she snapped. Next day Millicent's 'touchiness' was shown to be well-founded. Out on a walk we were passed by an older group of white students going in the opposite direction. 'I see the boat's come in,' remarked one loudly to the unconcealed merriment of his fellows.

A worse incident occurred in the same school in the same year. Three black boys were cast, very much against their will, in a first year production of a play about Columbus as 'natives' of the Caribbean whose role was to stand on the stage, receive gifts from Columbus and say nothing. Predictably, when performed before the school this moment in the play evoked laughter; the choice of three black children looked calculated to present their race in a ridiculous light, since they constituted a comparatively small minority in the school, but I am sure it was not, whatever unconscious forces may have been at work. When the boys heard the production was to be that day, one of them ran home. He was subsequently fetched and caned — so hard that, in his own words written in his autobiography the following year, 'it near broke my little finger and it went purple and bad'. The teachers involved were, incidentally, amongst the kindest and most dedicated I have known.

Frankly, I do not know what to do about this second form of teacher racism, but I have a suspicion that the kind of support and understanding I have argued for in the case of white racist children would do more good than the compulsory retraining programmes in multiracial education so loudly trumpeted by some classroom outsiders.

So to the most vexed question of all — how does one set about influencing the rest of the school, given that one has achieved some success in one's own classroom? Those who put this question frequently have in mind the many, often young and inexperienced teachers, in primary schools who feel isolated and frustrated by their inability to affect general policy, and find their own classroom initiatives jeopardised by the indifference or antipathy of their colleagues. There is little I can usefully say to them, beyond encouraging them to have faith in their own convictions and trust in their classroom relationships. At least in secondary schools, heads of departments have a certain amount of built-in influence; and even probationers in an average size comprehensive have a good chance of joining an informal group of like-minded colleagues from whom to derive ideas and support.

Whole school change is obviously going to be very much easier in innovative schools with institutionalised structures for curriculum development which, in theory at any rate, should guarantee an openness to fresh initiatives, however humble their source. I have been invited to address the staffs of a number of secondary schools in London and the West Midlands which have either mounted their own in-service programmes in multiracial education, or established working parties (in each case led by the deputy head) to examine the curriculum and organisational issues involved.

With or without machinery of this kind, there are one or two principles to observe which apply to all development across the whole curriculum. The most important is that on no account must teachers be placed in the position, if only by implication, of being told what they should and should not be doing. I would resist such an imposition as much as anyone else, whatever the content of the recommendation. This is a matter of rights as well as tactics. Teachers, like pupils, are entitled to expect to be shielded from the arrogance of the ideologues who believe that they alone have travelled the road to Damascus.

Given, however, that one has achieved something in the classroom, it is natural and proper to want to share findings and insights with colleagues, in the hope that this will lead to debate and development. It has of course to be conceded that, as far as multiracial education is concerned, the sharing of classroom experience may have just the opposite effect. Many of my former colleagues would find much of the children's writing I have quoted as more than ample justification for *not* developing a multiracial curriculum.

This book was conceived as an apologia for liberalism, in the classroom and outside. Those of us who espouse the liberal ideology (I have never been under the illusion that it was anything else) have had to put up too long with the cheap slur 'white liberal'. As Paul Johnson so cogently argues in the epilogue to *The Offshore Islanders* (Penguin), what Britain and the world need is more liberalism, not less. Ours is not a pusillanimous stance. We are as concerned about the fortunes of minority race children and as committed to the cause of multiracial education as the devotees of any other ideologies. Liberalism is founded on, amongst other things, optimism (I do not mean it is a liberal preserve) — optimism in this case about the future of the multiracial classroom; that it can become a place where pride in race is affirmed, and where interracial friendship and understanding are celebrated.

Notwithstanding all the tensions and animosities, all the negative and divisive outside pressures, the generation at present in our multiracial schools are already showing signs of growing up, in a way my generation never experienced, to accept and appreciate the multiracialness of Britain, and possessed of an unshakeable sense of their rights and of the common humanity which binds us all. On this generation I pin my hopes. My only doubt is whether we in the teaching profession can match them.

References

1   *Cause for Concern: West Indian Pupils in Redbridge* (Redbridge CRC), as summarized in the *New Statesman* (May 26, June 2nd) and the *Times Educational Supplement* (June 23rd).
2   From 'Talking and writing about race' by John Richmond *Multiracial School* Spring 1978.
3   *Multiracial School* Winter 1977.

Further Reading

Unlike the general areas of race relations and the history and cultures of British racial minorities, which lie outside my brief and my competence, there is precious little written about teaching in the multiracial classroom worth reading. The only good book, notwithstanding the reservations expressed about it in the last chapter, is Chris Searle's compilation *The World in a Classroom* (Writers and Readers Publishing Cooperative). Four articles I would strongly recommend are: 'Why Language Matters' *Multiracial School* Summer 1977 and 'The Core Curriculum and Multiracial Schools' *Multiracial School* Winter 1977 both by Alan James, Margaret Nandy's 'Social Studies for a Multiracial Society' in *The Multiracial School* eds. J. McNeal and M. Rogers (Penguin), and Mary Worrall's 'Multiracial Britain and the third world — tensions and approaches in the classroom' *The New Era* March/April 1978.

As for the teaching of English the whole of *English in Education* Spring 1977 is devoted to English in a multicultural society. I have referred to the two valuable articles by Joan Goody and Hugh Knight in chapter 5; there is a third in the issue which breaks new ground interestingly, Ranjana Ash's 'Introducing South Asian literature', and a useful booklist of West Indian writing for secondary schools at the end. More generally the NAME journal, *Multiracial School* and London NAME's broadsheet *Issues in Race and Education* often carry articles on different aspects of teaching in the multiracial classroom. *Multiracial School* has recently changed its name to *New Approaches in Multiracial Education*. Anyone interested in the National Association for Multiracial Education and/or its publications should write to Madeleine Blakeley, 23 Doles Lane, Findern , Derby DE6 6AX.

I have argued in chapter 4 that linguistics should be a mandatory element in the training of English teachers. Readers feeling themselves ill-equipped in this area will find David Crystal's *Linguistics* (Penguin) as good an introduction as any. Peter Trudgill's *Accent, Dialect and the School* (Arnold) is excellent on my preoccupations in the concluding section of chapter 4, although I have heard it described as 'extremist' by an English adviser, and Viv Edwards takes up the issues in relation to West Indian children in *The West Indian Language Issue in British Schools* (Routledge).
    On teaching English as a second language June Derrick's *Teaching English to Immigrant Children* (Longman) has become something of a classic, whilst her more recent overview *The Language Needs of Minority Group Children: Learners of English as a Second Language* (NFER) examines topical questions such as bilingualism as well.

Teachers concerned to define their own positions, in the manner of chapter 1, will find much of what they need to know of the national picture in David Smith's *Racial Disadvantage in Britain* (Penguin) and David Milner's *Children and Race* (Penguin), although both are already inevitably somewhat out of date. Otherwise the children themselves, their parents and the local communities remain the best sources of information; it is only a matter of keeping the channels of communication open. Complete newcomers to the field of multiracial education could do worse than make a start on the multiracial and black literature mentioned in the last three chapters of this book and the Spring 1977 issue of *English in Education*.

The fullest bibliography remains appendix 3 of the as yet unpublished report of the Schools Council project Education for a Multiracial Society.

'The major educational issue of our time is our failure to achieve an education which is equally available to all members of the various sub-cultures which constitute our society.... It would be unrealistic to expect inter-class and inter-ethnic inequalities to be solved in schools when they are so deep-rooted in economic and political inequalities, but this does not absolve teachers from the responsibility for action.'

Douglas Barnes *From Communication to Curriculum*

'My generation was always taught that black was dirty and white was clean. We were taught about the Black Hole of Calcutta, The Zulu War, and all those atrocities perpetrated by the coloured people. That was what our education was about and now, when the country's being flooded with coloureds, we've got to go and revise all our ideas.'

Secretary of Working Men's Club Wolverhampton

for all my pupils in Bristol, Mombasa, Wolverhampton and Birmingham.

Published 1979 by Writers and Readers Publishing Cooperative, 9-19 Rupert Street, London W1V 7FS in association with Chameleon, 22 Bicester Road, Richmond, Surrey.

Printed and bound in Great Britain by Staples Printers Limited, London, Rochester.

case ISBN 0 906495 02 4
paper ISBN 0 906495 03 2

Positive Image
Towards a multiracial curriculum

Robert Jeffcoate

Writers and Readers Publishing Cooperative
in association with **Chameleon**